Indian Immigrant Women and Work

In recent years, interest in the large group of skilled immigrants coming from India to the United States has soared. However, this immigration is seen as being overwhelmingly male. Female migrants are depicted either as family migrants following in the path chosen by men, or as victims of desperation, forced into the migrant path due to economic exigencies.

This book investigates the work trajectories and related assimilation experiences of independent Indian women who have chosen their own migratory pathways in the United States. The links between individual experiences and the macro trends of women, work, immigration and feminism are explored. The authors use historical records, previously unpublished gender disaggregate immigration data, and interviews with Indian women who have migrated to the US in every decade since the 1960s to demonstrate that independent migration among Indian women has a long and substantial history. Their status as skilled independent migrants can represent a relatively privileged and empowered choice. However, their working lives intersect with the gender constraints of labor markets in both India and the US. Vijaya and Biswas argue that their experiences of being relatively empowered, yet pushing against gender constraints in two different environments, can provide a unique perspective to the immigrant assimilation narrative and comparative gender dynamics in the global political economy.

Casting light on a hidden, but steady, stream within the large group of skilled immigrants to the United States from India, this book will be of interest to researchers in the fields of political economy, anthropology, and sociology, including migration, race, class, ethnic and gender studies, as well as Asian studies.

Ramya M. Vijaya is a Professor of Economics at Stockton University, New Jersey, US. Besides courses in Economics, she also teaches in the interdisciplinary Global Studies Minor.

Bidisha Biswas is Professor of Political Science at Western Washington University, US. She previously served as a policy adviser on South Asia to the United States Department of State.

Routledge Studies in Asian Diasporas, Migrations and Mobilities

Indian Immigrant Women and Work

The American experience

Ramya M. Vijaya and Bidisha Biswas

Routledge
Taylor & Francis Group

LONDON AND NEW YORK

First published 2017 by Routledge

2 Park Square, Milton Park, Abingdon, Oxfordshire OX14 4RN

52 Vanderbilt Avenue, New York, NY 10017

Routledge is an imprint of the Taylor & Francis Group, an informa business

First issued in paperback 2019

British Library Cataloguing in Publication Data
A catalogue record for this book is available from the British Library

Library of Congress Cataloging in Publication Data
Names: Vijaya, Ramya Mahadevan, 1974– author. | Biswas,
    Bidisha, author.
Title: Indian immigrant women and work : the American
    experience / Ramya M. Vijaya and Bidisha Biswas.
Description: Abingdon, Oxon ; New York, NY : Routledge, 2016. |
    Series: Routledge studies in Asian diasporas, migrations and
    mobilities ; 2 | Includes bibliographical references and index.
Identifiers: LCCN 2016028560 | ISBN 9781138690196
    (hardback) | ISBN 9781315537122 (ebook)
Subjects: LCSH: Foreign workers, East Indian—United States. |
    Women foreign workers—United States. | Women, East
    Indian—Employment—United States. | Women immigrants—
    Employment—United States. | India—Emigration and
    immigration—Economic aspects. | United States—Emigration
    and immigration—Economic aspects.
Classification: LCC HD8081.E3 V55 2016 |
    DDC 331.4089/91411073—dc23
LC record available at https://lccn.loc.gov/2016028560

ISBN: 978-1-138-69019-6 (hbk)
ISBN: 978-0-367-88960-9 (pbk)

Typeset in Times New Roman
by Apex CoVantage, LLC

Contents

Illustrations

Figures

Tables

Foreword

August 26th, Ottawa International Airport. As I lifted my two very heavy suitcases off the luggage carousel, I was excited about my new life adventure as a graduate student of engineering in Canada. It also meant I was now completely independent and on my own for the very first time in my life – no family or friends as safety net, no familiar surroundings or experiences to draw upon. I was a little scared but also very excited. I was looking forward to exploring a new land and culture, making new friends and pursuing professional growth with the help of a full scholarship. Growing up in a middle-class Indian family with parents who pushed both their girls to pursue higher education and independence was a great starting point. As the first member of my extended family to pursue higher education outside India, I was charting a new course and, in the long run, enabling many in my family to experience life in new contexts. As I stepped into this next phase of personal and professional growth, I had many questions and doubts: Will I succeed in this new culture? How will I change as a person? Do I have what it takes to use this springboard and carve a new path forward?

The story of immigration, as well as the challenges that come with it, is a familiar one. Throughout the ages humans have answered their inherent spirit of curiosity and adventure to push their comfort boundaries and explore new worlds, all with the aim of improving their quality of life. While immigrants, and women in particular, face multiple hurdles and pressures – community, social, financial, educational and cultural – it is their positive spirit, innovativeness and resourcefulness that have furthered the exchange of ideas and acceptance in new cultures.

In an innovative study, Ramya Vijaya and Bidisha Biswas explore the implications of these barriers on immigrant women from their native land of India and the progress they have made in their adopted country, the United States of America. During their research, Ramya and Bidisha found causes to celebrate victories great and small – from Anandibai Joshi being the first Indian woman to receive a medical degree anywhere in the world to

Ayesha being the first woman in her ultra-traditional family to embark on her independent journey and seek a new life in the United States. These uplifting, heart-warming stories document how each woman in her own way has broadened the viewpoints of people in her home and adopted countries. At the same time, the authors carefully illustrate structural and societal challenges that many women immigrants face as they carve out their professional paths. A key takeaway is that progress is not instantaneous or dramatic but rather happens over long periods of time. Shifts in mindset, acceptance and opportunities are often achieved through a series of small and subtle changes ("micro-negotiations"), each building on the previous one.

Over the decades, the numbers of Indian women independently migrating to the United States increased. However, these women continue to face many challenges in assimilating into the new culture while maintaining their individual and diverse make-up. Ramya and Bidisha trace the root causes in their extensive interviews and research and put forth some thought-provoking hypotheses to break the proverbial glass ceiling. As The Third Billion[1] rises in prominence and is expected to greatly influence the global economy by 2020, stories told in this book can empower Indian women to take up new challenges and make their mark internationally.

I have closely followed Ramya and Bidisha on their journey, as they defined the scope of their study, completed interviews, undertook archival research, responded to peer reviews and finally completed this book. At each step, I found them to be energized and excited to be the conduit for sharing both the individual stories they uncovered and in drawing linkages to broader issues. They have made a tremendous effort to bring to the reader the *real* voice of each woman featured in this book. As a fellow Indian immigrant, I saw glimpses of my experiences in many journeys and felt a connection with each of these women. I feel privileged to have been part of this unique and uplifting journey and believe that you will enjoy reading this book as much as I did.

— K. R. Prabha, Director, PwC Strategy& US,
based in Seattle, WA

Note

1 *The Third Billion* is the term used to represent the approximately one billion women in both developing and industrialized nations whose economic lives have previously been stunted, underleveraged, or suppressed, and who could, over the next decade, take their place in the global economy as consumers, producers, employees, and entrepreneurs. See Aguirre, DeAnne and Karim Sabbagh. 2010. "The Third Billion." *Strategy+Business*. http://www.strategy-business.com/article/10211?gko=98895 (accessed April 28, 2016).

Acknowledgements

Many have walked with us on the journey to complete this book. We are very grateful to K R Prabha, who has helped us in countless ways. The project has benefited from insightful conversations with Vicki Hsueh, Sunila Kale, Alka Kurian, Ranjit Arab, and Kavita Garg. We are grateful to our families for their unwavering support and counsel in all our endeavors.

Our home institutions, the Richard Stockton College of New Jersey and Western Washington University (WWU), have provided us with nurturing intellectual homes, ones which wholeheartedly supported a work that crosses several disciplinary boundaries. The office of Research and Sponsored Programs (RSP) at WWU provided us with generous funding to help complete the project. We have had the good fortune to work with the editorial and production team at Routledge.

We dedicate this book to the women who opened up their lives and journeys to us. Their spirit, perseverance, and candor enrich us in more ways than we can enumerate. We hope that this project is worthy of their inspiring stories.

Ramya Vijaya and Bidisha Biswas

1   Introduction

Marking a place in history

Breaking the mold

"Did your sister get married?"

"No, she went to the US because she got a job there."

In 1994, when her sister migrated to the US as a single woman, Ramya had several such conversations with friends, neighbors and acquaintances in India. The revelation that a middle-class woman in her early twenties chose to migrate in order to pursue her professional ambition would often be met with curiosity, suspicion, awe or some element of doubt. Through the late 1990s and into the new millennium, as both of the authors of this book and many of their contemporaries made their way to universities and jobs in the US, a hint of rebellion and a sense of being aberrations from the norm remained. What surprised us further was that the reactions we encountered in the US were usually no less incredulous. "Are you married? Do you have any family here? Did you really come here by yourself?" were questions that were often asked of us in our initial post-migration encounters.

At first, our stories of independent immigration seemed to be at the fringes of the Indian immigrant experience in the United States. In both countries, we seemed to not fit the preconceived notions about choices that women make. Immigration, in particular, has a tendency to be viewed as a male choice. Narratives about women migrants are usually narrow. They are depicted either as family migrants following in the path chosen by men or they are victims of desperation, forced into the migrant path due to economic exigencies. In writing this book, we are seeking to explore the experiences of women who have chosen their own migratory pathways. We came to discover that stories like ours, while not often recounted, in fact have a long and substantial presence in the history of Indian immigration to the US. While acknowledging a long history of early Indian visitors dating back to the 19th century, our book focuses on the stories of the contemporary, post 1965-generation of independent women migrants. Aided by a seminal change in US immigration policy in 1965, it is this generation that has been able to exercise the choice to create new working lives and immigrant histories in the US. In presenting these stories, we hope to expand narratives about immigrant women and their professional trajectories. These stories also allow us to examine comparative perspectives on gendered expectations and the incremental processes of empowerment and agency in a global context.

A unique combination of access to higher education and a long history of gender activism has made it possible for certain groups of Indian women to use immigration as a way to negotiate and challenge entrenched expectations about women's careers and life choices. Post-migration, they continue to encounter different but similarly rooted standards of gendered norms and expectations. Multilayered glass ceilings of race and gender present new challenges that must be navigated as Indian women discover that narrow images of women of color in the US have implications for their ability to find voice and visibility. The experiences of Indian women who are empowered by their professional and educational skills to make independent migration choices and yet are constrained by their gender in both countries provides a unique perspective to the evolving notions of gender dynamics in the workforce. It also enables an examination of new ways in which the assimilation experiences of relatively skilled immigrant groups of color impact the gender, race and class dynamics in the United States.

The individual journeys of our women and their micro-level negotiations to expand beyond the entrenched expectations for their gender and race are situated within the larger macro-level movements for gender equality in both countries. In some cases, we see that the macro movements have set the stage for these individual negotiations. In many cases, we also find that the individual journeys contribute to the incremental changes and debates in the larger macropolitics of gender empowerment. Highlighting these less recounted stories, therefore, expands the narrative about migration, gender and work. We also hope that it inspires and motivates our readers to see the possibilities for being agents of change through everyday choices.

A long unacknowledged history

> "My health is good, and this, with that determination which has brought me to your country against the combined opposition of my friends & caste . . ."[1]

In her letter seeking admission to the Women's Medical College of Pennsylvania in the year 1883, Anandibai Joshi (Figure 1.1) makes her pioneer status clear. Her journey to the United States to study medicine in the late

October 10, 1885

Dr.Anandabai Joshee,Seranysore,India
Dr. Kei Okami, Tokio, Japan
Dr. Tabat M. Islambooly,Damascus,Syria

Figure 1.1 Anandibai Joshi with fellow students at the Women's Medical College
of Pennsylvania.

Source: Legacy Center Archives, Drexel University College of Medicine

19th century was one that her friends or her larger caste community could not comprehend, let alone support. Nevertheless, she did make that controversial journey by herself and in 1886 became the first Indian woman to obtain a medical degree anywhere in the world.[2]

Other pioneering women followed in the footsteps of Anandibai Joshi. Gurubai Karmarkar from the American Marathi Mission in Bombay began her medical studies at the Women's Medical College in Pennsylvania in 1888.[3] At the University of Michigan, E K Janaki Ammal obtained her master's in botany in 1925. Born in 1897 in Tellicherry Kerala, Janaki Ammal graduated from Presidency College in Madras before securing a Barbour Scholarship for Oriental Women at the University of Michigan.[4]

Established in 1914 at the bequest of a former alumnus, Levi L. Barbour, the Barbour Scholarship was an important conduit for Asian women seeking to pursue higher education in the US. The scholarship was specifically intended to provide Asian women with the opportunity to get a western education. Soon after Janaki Ammal, in the 1928–29 academic year, Sharkeshwari Agha from Allahabad was granted the Barbour Scholarship. Having already received a master's degree from the University of Allahabad, Ms. Agha was principal of a high school before moving to Michigan.[5]

In the path of these early pioneers, a steady stream of Indian women have made their way, on their own, to the United States to study, to work and to create new independent lives. However, while Anandibai Joshi's story is known through a few academic works, the history of Indian women seeking their own paths who followed her remains largely untold. The story of Indian immigration to the US, in the common contemporary telling, is centered round a few narrow threads. The most prominent of these is the successful professional – a doctor, information technology worker, or a graduate student in science and technology fields. Interspersed amongst these tales of highly skilled and class-privileged Indians are stories of small entrepreneurs – the motel and convenience store owners made visible in popular culture. In this telling, the primary immigrant actors are men – Indian men coming to study science and technology in US universities, Indian men making up large numbers of the sought-after technology labor force, Indian men owning small businesses. It is the story of Apu, the Indian man who runs the Kwik-E-Mart in the iconic pop-culture TV show, *The Simpsons*.[6] And then there is Apu's wife, Manjula. Manjula is crucial to the story, but her significance lies in being Apu's wife and the mother of his eight children. Her story, like most accounts of immigrant Indian women, is a sideshow to the story of the primary immigrant actor.

Author Jhumpa Lahiri places women at the center of iconic stories of Indian immigrants. In her stories, the isolation of the young immigrant wife is a recurring theme. She poignantly describes the loneliness of women who begin their immigrant journeys being entirely dependent on their part-ners, with limited contact with the new environment.[7] In works that have captured the popular imagination, we see Indian women struggling to find the balance between assimilation and preserving cultural identity. This is undoubtedly an important story – but one that begins only *after* men have chosen the immigrant path.

The secondary status afforded to the stories of women immigrants is not unique to the Indian immigrant experience. Women's immigrant experiences have a long history of being ignored globally. Studies on migration focused exclusively on men until the late 1970s, with the unconfirmed assumption that women migrants constituted very small numbers.[8] Beginning in the late 1970s and early 1980s the newly emerging field of feminist scholarship began to pay attention to women's immigrant experiences.[9] This early focus on women immigrants remained on the fringes as special case studies. The overriding assumption that migrants were mostly male remained.

This assumption, in fact, had no statistical basis. Data on international migration were not disaggregated by gender till 1998. It was in this year that the United Nations Population Division released the first gender disag-gregated data estimates for immigrant populations for the years 1965–90. Using the estimates for foreign-born populations from country-level cen-sus surveys, the UN estimates indicated that women constituted nearly half (46.6 percent) of the total number of international migrants as early as 1960. Women continue to constitute nearly half of the migrant population worldwide.[10]

With the data undeniably underscoring the true gender trends, the false assumption about migration being a primarily male concern had to neces-sarily give way. The assimilation experiences of immigrant women, the gendered context of post-immigrant identity formation and the gender pat-terns in immigrant work have received much-needed attention in recent years. Yet the omission of assumptions regarding women migrants persists in different ways. While broad data trends have made it hard to ignore women's stories, their experiences continue to be narrowly presented in cases where more nuanced data remains missing. In the case of Indian immigrants to the US, the commonly presented narrative that men make the choice while women follow as families or associational migrants is not supported by data. The Year Book of Immigration Statistics published annually by the Department of Homeland Security[11] gives us the numbers to evaluate immigration trends in the US. But the yearbook numbers are in aggregate form and do not give separate information about men and women in the different immigrant categories. It is perhaps this lack of data that has obscured the long history of independent migration by Indian women. Our book seeks to move beyond this assumption of omission and expand the narrative by charting the long and substantial history of Indian women who are non-associational, independent migrants who choose to immigrate of their own volition.

In numbers: tracing the history of independent Indian women immigrants

Since the uncovering of relevant data has been important in breaking down assumptions about gender and migrations, we began our research by pursuing more detailed data about Indian immigrants in general and women in particular. We pick up the story in 1965. It is in this year that a crucial change in the US immigration laws fully opened the doors to immigrants from India and other non-European countries. Prior to 1965, a long history of various explicitly racists laws restricted Indian immigration to the US. The Naturalization Act of 1790[12] specifically restricted the right of naturalization to a "free white person." Unable to qualify as "white people," Indians were mostly limited to temporary visitor status in the US.[13] Women like Anandibai Joshi, Gurubai Karmarkar and E. K. Janaki Ammal returned to India after completing their studies. Even if some of the women might have wanted to stay on and create immigrant lives, the pre-1965 immigration system offered them very few pathways to permanent migration.

The Immigration and Nationality Act of 1952 finally made all races eligible for immigration and naturalization.[14] However, immigration from India continued to be restricted due to the national origins system, where immigration was based on quotas assigned to each nation. A majority of the quota was reserved for Western European countries. As a result, the national origins system heavily restricted immigration from Asia, Latin America and Africa.

By the 1960s, the civil rights movement made it hard to ignore the racist intent and impact of the national origins system.[15] Moreover, as some scholars have pointed out, the needs of a changing economic structure also demanded a different kind of immigration policy.[16] The Immigration and Nationality Act of 1965, also called the Hart-Cellar Act, finally dismantled the national origins quotas. In its place, the system that we are familiar with today was put into place. Under this system, immigration sponsorship is based not on national origin but on the fulfillment of one of two major criteria – family reunification or having skills that are in short supply in the US economy.

The family reunification criterion allows immigrants who are already in the US to sponsor their immediate and extended family for immigration. Since few Indians had migrated to the US prior to 1965, it was the skilled labor criterion that provided the initial spark to Indian immigration to the US. To receive sponsorship on the basis of skills, immigrants and their employers have to show that the particular skills are essential to the US economy and that there are insufficient qualified US workers available for such work. By its very nature, this system favors high-skill individuals and, by extension, those who have class privileges in their home country to access high-skill education.

Indian scientists, engineers and doctors fed the rising demand for technical workers in the US in large numbers in the first decade of the new immigration system.[17] Then came the family members of these skilled workers. Extended family followed the immediate family, and the Indian immigrant stream swelled. By the 1970s, the family-sponsored immigrants started to outnumber the employment-sponsored skilled immigrants. The absence of published gender disaggregated numbers has led to the common misperception that while most Indian men choose the migration path through work, Indian women mostly follow as family migrants.

We therefore pursued the numbers to get the full picture of what brings Indian women as immigrants to the US. On special request, we received previously unpublished gender-differentiated Indian immigrant data from the Department of Homeland Security for the years 1973–2012. The numbers are indeed illuminating. As Figures 1.2 and 1.3 show, for the years 1973–2012, 32 percent of all Indian women immigrants obtained their permanent immigration status through the employment criterion. When we compare these numbers to immigrant Indian men we see that the pattern is very similar: 37 percent of all Indian men during this same period were employment-sponsored immigrants. A greater proportion of both Indian men and women are family based-immigrants, but the numbers of work-sponsored men and

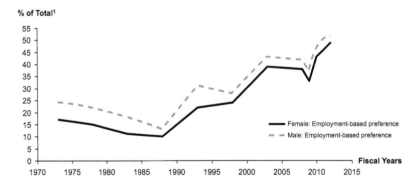

Figure 1.2 Employment-based permanent resident status by selected country of birth (India), major class of admission, sex (totals: Female: 267,199; Male: 301,442)

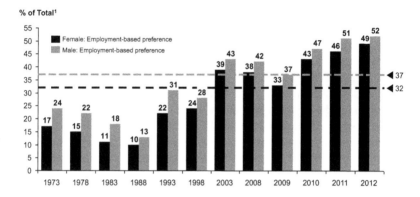

Figure 1.3 Employment-based permanent resident status by selected country of birth (India), major class of admission, sex (totals: Female: 267,199; Male: 301,442)

women are, contrary to popular conceptions, comparable. In more recent years the numbers in the work-sponsored category have increased for both men and women. In 2012, nearly half of the Indian women immigrants relied on work as the path to immigration. Based on this information, we can conclude that, for Indian women, work and professional opportunities are at least as important a motivator for moving to the US as marriage and family. This significant point has been neglected in much of the existing literature on Indian immigrant experiences.

Expanding narratives, exploring choice and agency

By ignoring women's experiences all together, the pre-1970s immigration studies were incomplete in their understanding of immigrant journeys and its impact on both the sending and receiving countries. Similarly, when stories about immigrant women's experiences are narrowly presented, we miss the opportunity to understand many aspects of daily struggles and choices that challenge existing norms and create change. In the absence of numbers, the experiences of non-associational Indian immigrant women have been lamentably ignored. As relatively empowered professional women from the third world who navigate entrenched expectations about gender roles in two different environments, their experiences can expand our understanding of the way women use their own agency to expand their choices and effect change. Feminist scholar Chandra Talpade Mohanty has notably pointed to the importance of expanding narratives to better understand this micropolitics of change. Mohanty argues that the experiences of women from the third world are, in particular, very narrowly presented.[18] As a result, we often fail to recognize the agency of the women themselves to effect change in their lives and in the larger socio-economic contexts globally.

The understanding of choice and agency generally tends to follow two extreme narratives. In the traditional economic approach, choice is understood as a result of rational cost-benefit calculations. Individual agents make choices that bring them the greatest level of satisfaction. An extension of this rational choice theory includes decisions made by families in the aggregate. Families are expected to make choices that will bring about the greatest combined level of satisfaction for all members. The decision about what will bring the greatest level of satisfaction and how that satisfaction is evaluated is entirely up to the individual (or the family) and is not the subject of analysis.[19] There is, therefore, no room for the kinds of social norms and customs that might enforce certain restrictive notions about choices and about what might bring the greatest level of satisfaction. For example, women might be conditioned to expect that prioritizing marriage and family over professional success is the right choice to make and will bring them the highest level of satisfaction.

Moreover, for ease of measurement, satisfaction in this economic calculus is usually evaluated in monetary terms. Prioritizing marriage over career might seem like a good monetary choice if women's wages are on an average lower than those of men. This of course does not allow for an exploration of the gendered social norms that perpetuate low wages for women. Similarly, if an individual (or family) chooses to emigrate, we might assume that immigration unambiguously brings greater monetary benefits than the cost of doing so. However, this narrow focus on the monetary benefits again obscures the different societal structures facing men and women. It leaves little room for understanding the kinds of prolonged negotiations and intergenerational coalitions that women build in order to overcome entrenched gendered barriers to making independent life and career choices. In fact, in many cases, the monetary rewards are not the only or even the primary motivation to choose migration for our group of already class-privileged migrant Indian women. Several women we spoke to described the desire to break away from restrictive gender roles or the desire to carry forward a certain tradition of barrier-breaking women in their own families or extended networks.

At the other extreme from the purely monetary evaluations, when the analysis of women's life choices centers overwhelmingly on the restrictive social and cultural contexts, there is a tendency to perceive women as being entirely voiceless. In this view, migration decisions of third world women are generally a symptom of dire economic compulsions or other exploitative socio-cultural factors, with limited agency assigned to the women. The possibilities of gaining greater voice and control over their decisions are explored only in their post-immigrant lives. Several gender and migration studies tend to look at what migration scholar Patricia R. Passar describes as the relationship between migration and emancipation.[20] As traditional family structures change and families attempt to establish new post-immigration assimilation routines, immigrant women, particularly those with jobs, tend to gain more control over domestic decision making. This stream of work highlights important dimensions of change in immigrant family structures and gender roles.

Yet viewing the pre-migration experience as uniformly exploitative and emancipation as largely a post-migration phenomenon tends to obscure the considerable history of vocal feminism and women's movements in the third world. It also assumes a linear progression of women's empowerment from the third world to the first world. This assumption perhaps explains the surprising initial reactions to our journeys we described in the first paragraph. Mohanty and other feminist scholars like Naila Kabeer have questioned this linear perspective, given that gendered constraints continue to be a feature of life and work globally. They instead argue for a more nuanced comparative perspective of what it means to be empowered in different contexts. The experiences of independent Indian women migrants are powerful as examples of this comparative perspective. Their journey serves as a forceful counterpoint to the linear narrative since they end up pushing the boundaries of women's choices regarding life and work in both their pre- and post-migrant contexts.

Pushing boundaries in both India and the US

Due to the specific context of US immigration policies, non-family women migrants from India usually make their way to the US as either students or skilled working professionals. Both of these represent relatively privileged and empowered choices when viewed against the broad landscape of women's economic opportunities in India. Only 29 percent of all women in India are currently employed or aim to be employed outside the home,[21] a very low rate even by the standards of most developing economies. According to the International Labor Organization, India ranks 11th from the bottom in terms of women's labor force participation among the total of 131 countries.[22] Add to this the persistent low literacy rates for women (65 percent compared to 82 percent for men, according to Census of India 2011)[23] and India continues to rank very low in global comparisons of gender equality.[24]

Given this backdrop, it is not only women of Anandibai Joshi's generation who are the pioneers. Each generation represents a path-breaking choice, a new dent in the ceiling placed on women's opportunities in one part of the world. Yet, in coming to the US, their journeys bring them to a country where a gender ceiling continues to persist. Even as she was helping Anandibai Joshi in her pioneering endeavor, Dean Rachel Bodley herself was breaking gender barriers as the first woman to hold the title of professor of chemistry in a medical college in the US.[25] Successful and barrier-breaking professional women in the US continue to debate the impact of the gender ceiling. Former Director of Policy and Planning for the United States Department Of State Anne-Marie Slaughter renewed the debate about the limitations to women's role in workplaces through her much-discussed 2012 article, "Why Women Still Can't Have it All."[26] Technology executive Sheryl Sandberg's 2013 book, *Lean In*, generated heated debates about the lack of women in leadership positions in Corporate America and about what women need to do to overcome barriers to their professional ascendancy.[27]

By some measures, the advances made by women in leadership positions in the US can fall short of the advances made by women in similar categories in India. As Figure 1.3 shows, in the often-cited gender gap index maintained by the World Economic Forum, the United States ranks 23 in overall index value, indicating a relatively high level of general gender equality. India ranks a distant 101. However, when the index components are viewed individually, the Indian ranking for political empowerment of women, measured by women's participation in elected office and political leadership roles, jumps to 9. The US ranking falls to 60.[28] Similarly, by

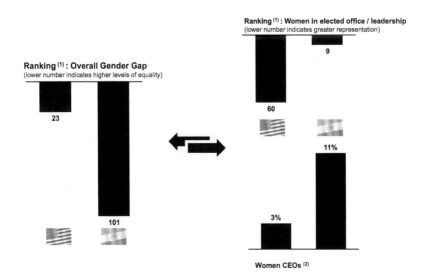

Figure 1.4 World Economic Forum Gender Gap Index comparison of India and US

some accounts, women represent 11 percent of the CEOs of Indian firms, whereas that number is only 3 percent for the US.[29]

We see this contrasting perspective reflected in the work trajectories we describe in this book. Often, immigrant Indian women have found that there are few women in their chosen fields of work in the US. As we will explore in later chapters, a combination of immigration requirements and the privileging of science and technology education for both men and women in India leads to a concentration of independent women migrants in fields of work where gender politics are an ongoing battle in the US. Their role as path breakers and trendsetters therefore continues post-migration. Their description of these post-migration battles raises interesting questions about what really constitutes change and progress in gender relations and how this change is achieved in an incremental manner by individual women.

The micropolitics of change

Here, the concept of micropolitics provides us with a valuable framework. Micropolitics encompasses everyday experiences and everyday practices and reveals processes by which an alternative socio-political order can be crafted by non-elites. It sidesteps the confining ideas about agency and choice being a primarily western or first world phenomenon by looking at ways in which everyday individual struggles and victories push the boundaries of women's empowerment and agency in all cultures. In our book, the professional experiences of women who occupy different positions in a variety of industries demonstrate how individual trajectories can contribute to a larger process of collective empowerment in the workplace. The women we study are agents of change because they are able and willing, in different ways, to challenge preconceived notions about their professional roles and contributions both in India and in the United States.[30] The discussion that follows draws important linkages between individual experiences and the larger, gendered dimensions of the American workplace. The stories that we present provide several strands of previously unexplored micropolitics. We present an overview of these themes here.

Different entry points, different struggles

Those who arrive in the US to seek professional opportunities will necessarily face a distinct set of experiences of immigration and assimilation than those who arrive on the basis of their familial links. When Anandibai Joshi stepped off the ship in New York, she was received and hosted by her American sponsor, Theodocia Carpenter. Subsequently, she was mentored by Rachel Bodley, the dean of the Medical College of Pennsylvania. With the Indian-born immigrant population totaling about 1.9 million in the latest census estimates,[31] contemporary immigrants are more likely to be greeted by a familiar face or at least have access to a wider network of Indian-born mentors upon immediate arrival. However, it is still the case that primary immigrants, workers or students, necessarily begin direct interactions with the new culture almost immediately.

Professors, co-workers and bosses are an expected part of the world that waits upon arrival. Speaking admiringly of his mother and aunt who came to the US as nurses, a second generation Indian American we encountered in the course of the research for this book mentioned, "They began working from week one." Uncertainties of culture and assimilation in this case might arise at a different pace and context than in the case of family sponsored immigrants. In the latter situation, the initial interactions with the new culture might be mediated by a spouse or other family members. Independent immigrants lack such a cushion. For Indian women, the immediate immersion into working life and culture is particularly challenging given the confusing gender expectations they are confronted with. In later chapters we see that there is a perception of meekness that tends to render Indian women invisible in the workplace. Many of our respondents described that challenging this perception and seeking out appropriate mentors is fraught with cultural confusion and suspicion. Interactions with the sizeable Indian immigrant community, particularly immigrant Indian men, are also uneasy. Here again, the challenge to the traditional roles assigned to Indian women that our group of women represents makes for a testy exchange. These tensions are an illustration of micropolitics that illuminates the intersections of race, class, gender and immigration in the workplace.

For example, one of the surprising observations we heard repeatedly was that the expectations and norms of femininity were more rigid and restrictive in the US in comparison to India. Our respondents reported that the US workplace places more emphasis on certain conceptions of physical appearance and grooming than Indian organizations. Such gendered experiences of relatively empowered women migrants in two different contexts allow us to compare the larger historical path of feminist movements in both countries and identify points of convergence and divergence.

Race, class and gender

In the US, workplace norms intertwine deeply with issues of class and race. The intersection of class, race and migration has been explored in the literature on Indian immigrants. In the book *American Karma*, social psychologist Sunil Bhatia (2007) observes that even affluent, highly skilled

Indian immigrants are transformed into "people of color" in the US. In the white-privileged racial hierarchy, "people of color" often hit a class plateau. That they can get so far but will not fit in at the very top is a perception that becomes hard to break.

In his influential book, the *Karma of Brown Folk*, sociologist Vijay Prashad has also argued that in the process of trying to overcome this perception, Indian immigrants have at times perpetuated and exacerbated aspects of racial privilege in the US.[32] The concentration of high-skilled individuals among independent Indian immigrants is a result of the specific provisions of the immigration system. Only workers with certain kinds of skills are allowed to negotiate permanent residency in this system. Yet Prashad describes how Indians are complicit in cultivating the idea that being skilled is an inherently cultural quality rather than an outcome of a specific policy bias. This false image of an inherently skilled "model minority" is often used by Indians to distance themselves from people of color, particularly African Americans, and align themselves more with "white" groups.

Neither Prashad nor Bhatia address the gendered aspects of migration and work. Sheba George (2005) has written one of the few studies that explore the stories of working Indian women migrants. Her book focuses on the experiences of nurse immigrants from the Syrian Christian community in Kerala. Her study however concentrates on a very specific subset of women immigrants. They do not represent the full spectrum of professional choices that Indian immigrant women have been making. It does not, therefore, situate the experiences of Indian women migrants within the gendered context of US workplaces.[33]

Even as the feminist movement in the US has pushed for greater opportunities for women in the world of work, it has often faced criticism for being too focused on the professional trajectories of middle-class women, who tend to be white. Historically, long before the visible entry of professional women in the workforce, African American women have had to work to support their families. The constricting norms of women and work in the 19th century meant that employment options for African American women were mostly in the domestic sphere as nannies and maids.[34]

As opportunities expanded for professional white women, they relied more and more on the domestic labor of poor and less empowered women of color who had few opportunities to make professional transitions. This increasing demand for domestic labor is now being filled by immigrant women of color. In the evocatively titled book *Global Woman: Nannies, Maids and Sex Workers in the New Economy*, Barbara Ehrenreich and Arlie Russell Hochschild[35] highlight the major trend in women's migration in recent years. Women of color from poorer countries are being driven by dire economic situations to leave home and seek employment as domestic workers in richer countries like the US. In fact, images of immigrant women in the popular culture in the US are mostly centered round their role as domestic workers. It is the Latina nanny who makes appearances in books, movies and TV shows. Depictions of migrant women of color in professional or leadership positions are mostly missing. Our book explicitly addresses this gap by situating India professional women at the center of this discussion.

Plan of the book: the stories we choose to tell

In this book we focus on the stories of the contemporary, post-1965 generation of independent women migrants. Aided by the seminal change in US immigration policy in 1965, it is this generation that has been able to exercise the choice to create new working lives and immigrant histories in the US. Over the course of about a year, we conducted structured interviews with 23 women. This, our core set of interviewees, left India as principal migrants for the purposes of work or study. All our respondents continue to remain in the US either as permanent residents, citizens or temporary workers hoping to transition to permanent status. All the respondents are currently engaged in work or study or are actively pursuing employment opportunities in the US.

We identified our interviewees through the snowballing technique, where we asked respondents to connect us to others who might fit our research criteria and be willing to speak to us about their experiences. As we expanded the circle of connections, we aimed for our final sample to have a wide representation of women from different regions in the US and India. The largest proportion of our respondents resided in the West Coast in the United States. This is followed by the New York and New Jersey Metropolitan area in the East Coast and then the Midwest. This mirrors the geographical spread of the Indian immigrant population in the US. California and the metropolitan regions of New York, New Jersey and Chicago have the three largest concentrations of Indian immigrants in the United States.[36] We also interviewed respondents residing in the southern states, where the immigrant Indian community has been expanding.

In choosing our sample we were conscious of representing women who migrated from different parts of India. In our respondent group we have migrants from the four largest metropolitan areas of India – Delhi (north), Chennai (south), Mumbai (west) and Kolkata (east). We also deliberately sought out immigrants from other cities in India, such as Hyderabad (south), Pune (west) and Bangalore (south). We note that there is an urban bias in our sample. We attempted to expand beyond the cities, and one of our earliest respondents is from a small town in the southern Indian state of Kerala. However, the clear trend in independent migration of relatively high-skilled women is that the majority of them are from larger cities and urban centers. A majority of the women we interviewed also self-identified as being from middle-class or affluent families. Most of them are also upper-caste Hindu. We spoke to a few women who identify as Christian or Muslim, and only one whose family belongs to a Scheduled Tribe. None of our respondents self-identified as being from a Scheduled Caste family.

We conclude that women whom we were able to interview come from families that had access to education and opportunities in India. The privilege of access helps explain the middle-class, urban and affluent bias in our sample as well as the upper-caste, Hindu skew. One of our respondents remarked that given our focus on independent migration, our cohort would necessarily have less variation in class: "Who else would have come on their own?" We were also reminded by one of our contacts that "Just the cost of applying to US universities can be prohibitive for one of modest means in India."

In subsequent chapters, we consciously address the class issues and other biases that this may represent. Notwithstanding the broad commonality of class characteristics of our women, there are still considerable variations among them. Individual stories differ in the level of privilege and empowerment that was accessible to women within their families. Some come with the support of families, others in opposition to family restrictions. Some are the first generation of women in their families to have a college education and a career. It is these gendered restrictions and the micropolitics they illustrate that motivate and inform our study.

We have endeavored to maximize the variation in age and professions among our respondent group. Our respondents include women who have arrived in the US in every decade since 1965. This range also ensured considerable variation in the professions. While the qualifying criterion for independent migration requires Indian women to be relatively skilled, the categories of skilled work that women are choosing have themselves expanded. While the early emphasis was on medicine and other science and technology fields, the more recent generations of immigrant Indian women represent a wider variety of occupations. During our research, we spoke to women in a number of professional roles, including human resources managers, business consultants, social scientists, nurses, therapists, and sales and marketing professionals. Of the 24 women we interviewed, the majority, but not all, were single at the time of their initial arrival to the US. Figures 1.5 and 1.6 depict the migration pathways, occupations and marital status of our respondents. Table A.1 in the Appendix provides more detailed information on them.

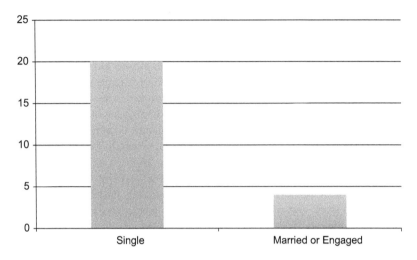

Figure 1.5 Marital status of respondents

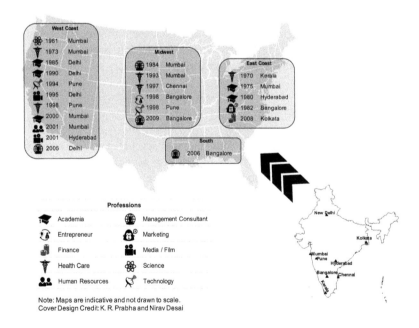

Note: Maps are indicative and not drawn to scale.
Cover Design Credit: K. R. Prabha and Nirav Desai

Figure 1.6 Migration pathways and occupations of respondents

While our study primarily focuses on independent migrants, we are cognizant of the fact that professional concerns are also central to the experiences of many women who have arrived in the US on associational/ dependent visa categories. In many cases the choice of migration status is merely incidental. Given immigration restrictions as well as familial expectations, an associational visa status can be the most feasible path to pursuing advanced studies and/or professional opportunities in the United States. We also recognize that many family sponsored immigrant women look for employment in order to augment their family income or adapt to changing family circumstances.[37] During the course of our research, we encountered a number of women who began their immigrant journeys on spousal visas but who remained focused on pursuing fulfilling professional opportunities. "Soon after arriving on a spouse visa, I switched to a student visa. I later got my own work visa when I started a job. In fact, I have covered pretty much ever category of visa there is!" explained one of our initial contacts. Another respondent pointed out that our "dataset also excludes women who have independent, successful careers, like my sisters, who came on family visas." In recognition of their potential role as agents of change, we interviewed five women who came on spousal or family visas and pursued professional pathways. While we did not include these women in our core sample, their experiences provided us with important insights in developing this book. Our concluding chapter explores some of our initial findings regarding the professional pathways of dependent women migrants. Table A.2 in the Appendix provides details on our ancillary set of dependent immigrant women.

The interviews

We followed a structured questionnaire that was developed prior to contacting our respondents. Each interview lasted about an hour. Given the geographical spread of our respondents, we did a mix of in-person and phone interviews. The primary purpose of this research is to highlight the professional trajectories of women who are path breakers in many ways and understand the processes that were involved in choosing and forging this uncommon path. Our questionnaire therefore focused on issues relating to their migration decision, work choices, family and workplace challenges and limitations both pre and post-migration. We also collected demographic information about our respondents and their families. The questionnaire is included in the appendix.

A majority of our respondents were well aware of their pioneer status and welcomed the opportunity to reflect on their journeys and the challenges of work, gender relations and life choices. In many cases, though, the challenges are ongoing, and concerns were expressed about keeping the sensitive nature of this discussion anonymous. We assured our respondents as we do our readers that we followed strict institutional review board protocols to protect the anonymity of our respondents and the information they provided. In the following chapters, as far as possible, we endeavored to retain the voices of the women themselves in telling their stories, but at the same time we ensured that all identifying information was removed. For the same reason we use aliases for all our respondents.

The flow of the book

In the next chapter we begin following the journeys of our group of independent migrants by looking at their motivations for migration. Despite the relative economic security of their middle-class backgrounds, we found that a majority of the women felt extremely constrained in their ability to make fulfilling life choices. The restriction of choice also seems to increase incrementally as the women complete their education and prepare for adult life. In varied voices, family and friends seem to reinforce traditional expectations of marriage and family after the relative freedoms allowed during their student years. The choice of migration often emerges, therefore, as a rebellion against these escalating restrictions. In this pushback against the limitations of choice, we see examples of a micropolitics; the ways in which change is affected by the everyday lived experiences of individuals questioning and challenging limitations. We also uncover a remarkable intergenerational transfer of aspirations, as many of our interviewees note that their mothers and other older women in their households supported and often nurtured their immigrant ambitions.

In addition to challenging conventional gender norms, migration is also motivated by considerable passion and enthusiasm for their area of work and study. Across generations, our cohort of women remembered the high expectations for the professional possibilities that they felt would be available to them in the US. In Chapters 3 and 4, we follow their post-migration journeys by comparing these high expectations against the post-migration realities of their professional lives in the US.

In Chapter 3 we see that the post-migration reality often involves encounters with a gender and racial glass ceiling. A specific combination of education policies in India and immigration imperatives in the US have led to the concentration of independent women migrants in fields of work where there are often few women at higher levels of the profession. Consequently, Indian women often seem to face a discrimination of assumptions based on racial and gendered stereotypes that challenge their career progression in various subtle ways. Interestingly, we also find that the combined impact of gender and race distinguishes Indian women's experiences from that of Indian men in US workplaces. In fact we see a fraught interaction between immigrant Indian men and women in the professional world.

In Chapter 4, we explore the ways in which Indian women have responded to the discrimination of assumptions and other subtle barriers of the glass ceiling. We uncover stories of spirited determination. While later cohorts of immigrants do seem to have access to support networks established by earlier migrants, the fact that our respondents work in environments where there are few women of color continues to be a limiting factor in the development of such networks. Their experiences offer a fresh perspective on the debate about individual responsibility for networking versus systemic and policy responses that support diversity at workplaces. Even as our group of women show considerable resourcefulness in building supportive networks, we also find that their efforts have been more successful when supported by organizational and policy initiatives.

In Chapter 5, we situate these experiences of Indian immigrant women within the parallel histories of feminist movements in both the India and the US. Most of our interviewees declared that they neither identified as feminists, nor did they consciously relate to a collective movement for women's opportunities before migration. Nevertheless, as we trace the history of feminism in India we see that a long and powerful tradition of women's activism dating to the 19th century has built the foundation that enabled the independent journeys of our women. Post-migration, as they encounter the racial and gender dynamics of US workplaces, a more activist spirit does develop among several women we spoke to. Given the complex race and class interactions within the history of the feminist movement in the US, Indian women have at times struggled to find a space within it. Yet, right from the early Indian visitors like Anandibai Joshi, we do see possibilities for developing a shared experience of feminism and a global women's compact.

We re-evaluate the broad trends observed in our study and present concluding thoughts in Chapter 6. We begin by tracing the history of Indian women immigrants who have reached a position of significant professional success and accompany fame. In their stories, which we narrate on the basis of secondary information, we see patterns of the larger fabric. This fabric includes our respondents, and we see shared experiences of cross-cultural miscommunication and eventual understanding; of the discrimination of assumptions and the successful challenges to those assumptions; of finding life partners who support the expansion, rather than narrowing, of choices; of consciously encouraging others – and, above all, of ambition, spirit, and resilience. The concluding chapter also narrates some initial findings based on our conversations with dependent women immigrants and their professional trajectories in the United States. We identify some points of convergence and divergence from our core sample, indicating a promising area for future research.

Conclusion

As a relatively new immigrant population, the documentation of the Indian American journey is at a nascent stage. As Indian immigrants to the US have rapidly increased in number and have recently achieved the status of the third largest immigrant group in the United States, their journeys have elicited increasing interest. High-skill specialty occupation workers, many of whom work in information technology related industries, have tended to dominate popular and policy attention. Their contribution to the US economy and the identification of a suitable immigration policy that accommodates their increasing numbers is a subject on which much has been written.[38]

An important theme in the explorations of the working lives of Indian immigrants is their encounters with the race and class dynamics in the US. The high-skilled backgrounds and occupations of some Indian immigrants can afford a certain immediate class privilege that in the past might have taken new immigrant groups a few generations to work towards. But the class privilege can be circumscribed by the realities of racial and gendered hierarchies in the US. As non-white immigrants, even second generation Indian Americans can be seen as 'outsiders' who have to manage their responses to certain preconceived notions about race and capabilities in the workplace.[39]

Recognizing that the existing body of literature on the subject has a gender bias, our study highlights the voices of the considerable number of women who have made work and study their primary motivation for their immigrant journeys. With a few notable exceptions, such as George's 2005 study of nurses from Kerala, their presence has remained unrecorded in most writings on the Indian American experience.

The forays of such women into the world of work in the US links the race and class discussions in the Indian immigrant literature to gender dimensions of race and class in the US. Research for this book helped us understand the evolving immigration and assimilation debates and experiences in the US. Exploring a diverse range of immigrant experiences is a valuable exercise because it presents multifaceted views on a wide variety of issues including ambition, work, exploitation, race and class. The less recounted stories of Indian women who make their own independent immigrant pathways offer a valuable and unique perspective on many different aspects of the immigrant experience.

As stories of empowerment and enterprise, these experiences are also worth highlighting in themselves. A second generation Indian American woman said to us, "It just occurred to me that I never really thought about how my mother made her way here." We hope that our explorations will reinforce the somewhat hidden reality that women do, in fact, exercise considerable agency in immigration choices. By recounting some of the stories of these path-breaking journeys we hope to motivate more such thinking and preserve a record of this unique history for the next generations.

Notes

1 Anandibai Joshi to Alfred Jones, June 28, 1883, a291_006, Materials Related to Rachel Bodley 1868–1991, The Legacy Center Archives and Special Collections (a291_006), Drexel University College of Medicine.
2 Joshi is also believed to be the first Hindu woman to set foot on American soil. http://www.pri.org/stories/2013–07–12/historical-photos-depict-women-medical-pioneers (accessed May 28, 2016).
3 Congregational Library. "Dr. Gurubai Karmarkar, M.D." *Congregational Library   Exhibits.*   http://exhibits.congregationallibrary.org/items/show/105 (accessed May 31, 2014).
4 Subramanian, C.V. 2008. "Edavaleth Kakkat Janaki Ammal." In *Lilavati's Daughters: The Women Scientists of India*, eds. Rohini Godbole and Ram Ramaswamy. Bangalore: Indian Academy of Sciences, 1–4.
5 Rufus, Carl W. 1942. "Twenty-Five Years of the Barbour Scholarships." *Michigan Alumnus Quarterly Review* 49 (11): 14–26.
6 The Simpsons is an animated television show that began in 1989. The long running show is a satire about family life in the US. It is often considered to be a reflection of popular culture and stereotypes in the US. See Carr, David. 2005. "Will the Simpsons' Ever Age?" *New York Times.* http://www.nytimes.com/2005/04/24/arts/television/24carr.html?pagewanted=1 (accessed June 2, 2014).
7 Lahiri, Jhumpa. 2003. *The Namesake*. New York: Houghton Mifflin; Lahiri, Jhumpa. 2013. *The Lowland*. New York: Knopf; Lahiri, Jhumpa. 2009. *Unaccustomed Earth*. New York: Vintage.
8 Zlotnik, Hania. 2003. "The Global Dimensions of Female Migration." *Migration Information Source*. Migration Policy Institute. http://www.migrationpolicy.org/article/global-dimensions-female-migration (accessed April 1, 2016).
9 Hondagneu-Sotelo, Pierrette. 2003. *Gender and U.S. Immigration: Contemporary Trends*. Berkeley: University of California Press.
10 Zlotnik 2003.
11 Previously published by the Immigration and Naturalization Service, Department of Justice.
12 An Act to Establish an Uniform Rule of Naturalization. 1790. 1st Cong., 2d Sess., Chap. 3.
13 In 1920, Bhagat Singh Thind, originally from Amritsar, India, applied for US citizenship after having served in the US army during World War I. However, his application was denied, and the case went all the way to the Supreme Court. In 1923, the Supreme Court of the United States clarified that Indians did not meet the qualifying criterion of being "white" ' and therefore ineligible for

naturalization and citizenship. See Halley, Jean, Amy Eshleman, and Ramya Mahadevan Vijaya. 2011. *Seeing White: An Introduction to White Privilege and Race*. Lanham, MD: Rowman & Littlefield for more information.
14 Bennett, Marion T. 1966. "The Immigration and Nationality (McCarran-Walter) Act of 1952, as Amended to 1965." *Annals of the American Academy of Political and Social Science* 367, The New Immigration (September): 127–136.
15 Kennedy, Edward M. 1966. "The Immigration Act of 1965." *Annals of the American Academy of Political and Social Science* 367, The New Immigration (September): 137–149.
16 Prashad, Vijay. 2001. *The Karma of Brown Folk*. Minneapolis, MN: University of Minnesota Press.
17 Liu, John M. 1992. "The Contours of Asian Professional, Technical and Kindred Work Immigration, 1965–1988." *Sociological Perspectives* 35 (4): 673–704; Prashad 2001.
18 Mohanty, Chandra Talpade. 1984. "Under Western Eyes: Feminist Scholarship and Colonial Discourses." *Boundary 2* 12 (13): 333–358; Mohante, Chandra Talpade. 2003. " 'Under Western Eyes' Revisited: Feminist Solidarity through Anticapitalist Struggle." *Signs* 28 (2): 499–535.
19 For more on the rational choice theory, please see: Kabeer, Naila. 2000. *The Power to Choose: Bangladeshi Garment Workers in London and Dhaka*. London: Verso; Ferber, Marianne A. and Julie A. Nelson. 1993. *Beyond Economic Man: Feminist Theory and Economics*. Chicago: University of Chicago Press.
20 Passar, Patricia R. 2003. "Engendering Migration Studies: The Case of New Immigrants in the United States." In *Gender and U.S. Immigration: Contemporary Trends*, ed. Pierrette Hondagneu-Sotelo. Berkeley: University of California Press, 20–43.
21 International Labour Organization. 2013. *Global Employment Trends 2013*. Geneva: International Labour Organization.
22 International Labour Organization. 2013. "India: Why Is Women's Labour Force Participation Dropping?" *ILO Newsroom*. February 13. http://www.ilo. org/global/about-the-ilo/newsroom/comment-analysis/WCMS_204762/lang—en/index.htm?utm_source=twitterfeed&utm_medium=twitter (accessed May 1, 2014).
23 Census of India. 2011. "Provisional Population Totals: India: Census 2011." http://censusindia.gov.in/2011-prov-results/indiaatglance.html (accessed June 2, 2014).
24 In the Global Gender Gap Index developed by the World Economic Forum, India ranked a low 101 out of 136 countries in 2013 (See World Economic Forum. 2013. *The Global Gender Gap Report 2013*. Geneva: World Economic Forum.). Similarly, in the United Nations Development Programme's Gender Inequality Index, India ranks 137 out of 195 (see United Nations Development Programme. 2013. *Human Development Report 2013*. New York: United Nations Development Programme).
25 Eric Rosenzweig. 2010. "Rachel L. Bodley Papers." Philadelphia Area Consortium of Special Collections Library. July 24. http://hdl.library.upenn. edu/1017/d/pacscl/DUCOM_WMSC420xml (accessed April 25, 2014).
26 Anne-Marie Slaughter. 2012. "Why Women Can't Have It All." *The Atlantic* July/August.
27 Sandberg, Sheryl. 2013. *Lean in: Women, Work, and the Will to Lead*. New York: Knopf.
28 World Economic Forum 2013.

29 Marston, Ama. 2013. "Are Women in the West Being Left Behind on Leadership?" *The Guardian.* http://www.theguardian.com/women-in-leadership/2013/oct/23/women-in-west-left-behind-leadership (accessed May 5, 2014).
30 For more on micropolitics, please see: Chakravarty, Anuradha. 2013. "Political Science and the 'Micro-Politics' Research Agenda." *Journal of Political Sciences and Public Affairs* 1 (1): e103; Herzog, Hanna. 2009. "Choice as Everyday Politics: Female Palestinian Citizens of Israel in Mixed Cities." *International Journal of Politics, Culture, and Society* 22 (1): 5–21; Mohante, Chandra Talpade. 2003. " 'Under Western Eyes' Revisited: Feminist Solidarity through Anticapitalist Struggle." *Signs* 28 (2): 499–535.
31 According to the 2012 American Community Survey Estimates there are 1,967,998 Indian-born individuals in the US. U.S. Census Bureau. 2012. *2012 American Community Survey 1-Year Estimates, Table B05006.* http://factfinder2.census.gov (accessed June 8, 2014).
32 Prashad 2001.
33 George 2005, p. 47.
34 Halley et al. 2011.
35 Ehrenreich, Barbara and Arlie Russel Hochschild. 2002. *Global Woman: Nannies, Maids and Sex Workers in the New Economy.* New York: Henry Holt.
36 Zong, Jie and Jeanne Batalova. 2015. "Indian Immigrants in the United States." *Migration Information Source,* Migration Policy Institute. http://www.migrationpolicy.org/article/indian-immigrants-united-states (accessed August 19, 2015).
37 Shah, Sonia. 1998. "Three Hot Meals and a Full Day at Work." In *A Patchwork Shawl: Chronicles of South Asian Women in America,* ed. Shamita Dasgupta. New Brunswick: Rutgers University Press, 206–222; Kalita, Mitra. 2005. *Suburban Sahibs.* New Brunswick: Rutgers University Press.
38 Hira, Ron. 2010. "The H-1B and L-1 Visa Programs Out of Control." *Economic Policy Institute Briefing Paper 280;* Kirkegaard, Jacob Funk. 2007. "The Accelerating Decline in America's High-Skilled Workforce: Implications for Immigration Policy." *Policy Analysis in International Economics, Institute for International Economics 84;* Banerjee, Payal. 2006. "Indian Information Technology Workers in the United States: The H-1B Visa, Flexible Production, and the Racialization of Labor." *Critical Sociology* 32 (2–3): 425–445; Chakravartty, Paula. 2006. "Symbolic Analysts or Indentured Servants? Indian High-Tech Migrants in America's Information Economy." *Knowledge, Technology & Policy* 19 (3): 27–43.
39 Prashad 2001; Dhingra, Pawan. 2007. *Managing Multicultural Lives: Asian American Professionals and the Challenges of Multiple Identities.* Palo Alto, CA: Stanford University Press; Bhatia, Sunil. 2007. *American Karma: Race, Culture and Identity in the Indian Diaspora.* New York: New York University Press.

2 Choosing to leave

Choices and the micropolitics of change

Acclaimed author Chimamanda Ngozi Adichie makes a strong case for expanding the narratives about immigrant experiences. In her insightful stories about Nigerian immigrants in the US, the protagonists tend to be from the middle class; often starting their immigrant journeys after acquiring college degrees. Adichie argues,

> When people think of African immigrants, they immediately think of poverty. I wanted to write about the type of immigration I am familiar with, an immigration of people who are not starving, who are middle class, who choose to leave because they want more choices.[1]

Adichie's writing offers us powerful insights into the nature of choices, aspirations and the evolving struggles of immigrant assimilation. The same inclination to diversify the discussion of immigrant experiences led us to investigate the trend of independent women migrants from India. Like Adichie's fictional characters,[2] in our respondents' stories we found fascinating journeys of expanding choices in work and life in the face of shifting gender and class norms.

Jaya had earned a bachelor's degree in biology in India. She lived with her family in Mumbai and earned a little bit of money in theater. Her family, as she describes them, was middle class. As she considered her personal and professional future, the options seemed limiting:

> I wanted to get into medicine, but there was not much opportunity in India, and I wanted to explore the newer field of medical technologies. [I] also did not want the pressure of an arranged marriage. I didn't want my parents to bear the burden of marriage expenses and all that.

In 1973, soon after the path-breaking 1965 Immigration Act, Jaya made her way to Philadelphia to pursue a degree in medical technologies. Two years later, with the degree completed, she left for Atlanta in search of better job opportunities. Jaya's immigrant journey continued to evolve, bringing with it the expanded choices for life and work that she had hoped for. She eventually met and married a person of her own choice and went on to set up a successful business in medical technologies.

When we look at existing narratives of immigrant women in the US, we rarely encounter stories of expanding choices. Women like Jaya, who exercise their own agency in search of professional opportunities, are not often chronicled. The increasing awareness that women constitute a little more than half the immigrant population has brought much-needed attention to the gender dynamics of immigration. But there is a tendency to converge on a few narrow, albeit important, themes. Many immigrant narratives now examine the struggle and exploitation of immigrant women of color in their role as service workers in the US.[3] Others focus on the changing gender roles within families as immigrants adapt to the uprooting of cultural contexts.[4] Studies of immigrant Indian women in the US focus mostly on this post-migration search for new identities and cultural contexts.[5]

In her seminal work on the representation of "Third World" women in western narratives, Chandra Talpade Mohanty argued that there is a tradition of propagating a singular image of weakness and powerlessness.[6] Glossing over different circumstances, lives of women of color from non-western backgrounds are often portrayed as uniformly oppressive, with no room for the exercise of individual choices. This one-dimensional portrayal often prohibits a more nuanced understanding of the varied nature of constraints that women from different backgrounds face. More importantly, it also obscures the stories of empowerment – the many ways in which women constantly push and challenge the constraints at various levels.

Other feminist writers have since echoed Mohanty's critique. In her well-regarded work, feminist author Naila Kabeer makes a similar argument against the narrow images of the struggles of women from developing economies. The exaggerated focus on the structural constraints that bind all women, Kabeer writes, leaves little room for understanding the ways in which women do exercise individual voice and agency in specific situations.[7]

The stories we explore, like that of Jaya, follow a thread that has rarely been explored. Jaya's migration choice came from the relative economic security of a middle-class background. Her experiences, successes and struggles were not the result of economic desperation. All of the women we interviewed come from families that would qualify to be categorized as the economic middle class in India. Middle class is a position of considerable privilege in India given the small numbers that this group constitutes.

For example, the National Council of Applied Economic Research in India identified that only about 13 percent of the total population, with the ability to spend between $8 and $40[8] per person per day, can be considered the middle class in India.[9] While we could not gather information on the incomes of the families of our respondents,[10] we used other asset-based indicators that have been used to assess economic class status. For example, economists Krishna and Bajpai consider the ownership of transport assets as an indicator of economic class.[11] Nearly 80 percent of Indian households own only a bicycle or have no vehicle at all. This implies that these households do not have the income capacity to qualify as middle class. About 17 percent of households who do own a motorcycle or a motorized scooter can be qualified as the economic middle class. Only about 2 percent of all households own a car, making them the most affluent group. In our group of women, only two reported that their families did not own at least a motorcycle or a scooter. A number of them reported that their families owned a car, and all of them self-identified as being either middle class, lower middle class, or affluent. None identified as being poor.

This economic security does not, however, tell us much about the gender relations within the households. Recent research continues to document considerable gendered constraints even within the economic middle class.[12] Only a small proportion, 30 percent, of women in the middle class have a bank account in their name, and a majority report having to ask for permission to step out of the house, even for routine errands. At the same time there is a strong history of feminist activism in India that has found varied ways to challenge gender norms in incremental ways across the economic classes. As we will see in later chapters, the Indian movement for women's empowerment emerged out of the middle-class movement for social reform in the mid-19th century. Over its long history it has at times paralleled and in some ways outpaced the women's movement in the US in its successes and setbacks. The choice of women like Jaya to migrate independently and to seek out the best professional opportunities possible represents a continuation of this considerable history of pushing against the boundaries of gender norms in the workplace and in society overall. Their stories expand the view of immigrant women as either voiceless victims of economic desperation or as family migrants who begin questioning gender roles only in their post-immigrant quest to reconcile cultural identity with assimilation.

In Jaya's choice to migrate and the migration choices of other relatively skilled immigrant women like her we see reflected the long tradition of everyday challenges that women use to bring about change at the micro level. This is the process that Mohanty refers to as the "micropolitics of everyday life." The micropolitics include the subtle and often varied nature of arguments, opposition and support that people continuously experience within their own families and immediate social network. While the larger themes of gender and inequality might seem to be overwhelming and all constricting, the micro-level constraints that different categories of women confront in their daily lives are not uniform and can include many subtle differences. These differences can give us a better understanding of not only the constraints themselves but also of the many small and large ways in which traditional boundaries are navigated and challenged. As we uncover more examples and widen the narrative, therefore, we get a better understanding of the possibilities and processes of change in the larger macropolitics of gender and empowerment.

So far, but no further

As we sought out the different motivations that led women to make the independent migration choices, we found several examples of the micropolitics of change. Like Jaya, many women we spoke to used the immigration choice as a way not only to expand economic choices but also to push against the limitations of gender and patriarchy in their personal lives.

Kavita came to the US in 2001 for a master's program when she was 26 years old. Explaining her decision to leave India, she describes independence and money, rather than education, as the primary motivators. "My parents were not restrictive, they gave me lots of independence, but I wanted more." Kavita had already completed a master's degree in India. She had a job and lived with her parents in Mumbai. Both her parents had master's degrees. Her mother had not worked outside the house, and she described her family as upper middle class. On further reflection, Kavita added "I was consciously a feminist when I arrived; it was about me asserting myself against my dad and his Punjabi family."

Just like Jaya in 1973, Kavita felt that the "more" was not possible within the family constraints of her life in India. After allowing a certain level of freedom, at least one branch of her family had constraining expectations of their daughter. With no financial support from her father, who actively opposed her move, Kavita applied for and received a full scholarship from the university in the US where she would pursue her master's program.

Starting from the earliest group of immigrant women, and in each successive generation, we found that many of the women we spoke to encountered this combined personal and professional wall in their early 20s. Most of our respondents said that their families were supportive and encouraging of their daughters' independence and educational pursuits – but only up to a point. Thereafter, the expectation of a traditional marriage and family becomes more important than career and independent personal choices. "You can go so far but no further, at least in India," seems to be the unchanged message that middle-class women receive from their families and extended social networks in each decade. Not only does this message seem to be consistent across the decades, but it also seems to recur in families from different parts of India. While both Jaya and Kavita are from the large metropolitan city of Mumbai in western India, women from other parts of India also mentioned facing similar expectations.

In 1985, nearly a decade after Jaya and a decade before Kavita, Mira, from the Indian capital of New Delhi, described being aware of this message from her larger social network. "I did see my friends get married in India, and I didn't want that," she remembers. So she left to pursue a graduate degree in the US. Similarly, Ayesha, from the southern Indian city of Bangalore, one of the youngest women we interviewed, encountered the same contradiction. Her family supported her educational pursuits, but she faced the constraints of traditional family expectations after obtaining her undergraduate degree.

By her own account, Ayesha's extended family was "very conservative."

> I was very protected in India: I was not even allowed to go down the street alone, girls were not to be heard in my family, it was assumed that they would be married right after education. I came to the US to experience a different life.

In 2011, Ayesha arrived in Philadelphia to pursue graduate studies – much like Jaya had in 1973.

Reena experienced that closing of options after graduation in a more personal manner. "My sister was married at 21, arranged at 17. I was in class 8. I was devastated by that, I did not want an arranged marriage." To escape what seemed like the inevitable path of narrowing personal choices in her early 20s, Reena decided to leave India in pursuit of professional opportunities. Unlike most of the other women we spoke to, however, she did not come directly to the United States. She moved to the United States after having spent three years studying and working in another country.

Reena's family accepted her pursuit of independence in stages. During her undergraduate years, she decided to stay in the university hostel even though her parents lived in the same city. This was an unconventional choice. Undergraduate students in India by and large continue living with their parents, particularly if they attend a university in the same city. Of her choice, Reena said, "I lived in the hostel to live away from parents." Her parents found themselves having to reconcile themselves to this decision.

Soon after completing her degree, Reena was offered a job in a different city in northern India. Allowing her to go away to an entirely different city required her parents to come a little further in accepting her independence. They reconciled themselves to the move since that job with a multinational corporation came with a salary that was hard to turn down. Reena describes her family as middle class with modest financial means. The well-paid multinational job would allow her to augment the family finances. Reena recalled, "They agreed to have me go since it paid very well."

Her family's willingness to accept her increasing independence, however, was put to the test when she received the scholarship to study overseas. Convincing her parents to accept a move to an entirely different country was more challenging. Her mother continued to be supportive, but her father "was not excited." But Reena would be able to send part of her scholarship money to her family. She not only continued to maintain her financial independence but also to support her family. Her mother, she recalls, was proud of her daughter's ability to augment their family income.

This gradual acceptance of Reena's growing independence within her family provides a powerful example of the kinds of micropolitics women navigate and use to effect change incrementally. In the face of new and expanding financial opportunities, Rita was able to increase her capacity to make independent choices. As they benefited from her financial success and took pride in her professional advances, Reena's family members also became more accepting of Reena's ability to make independent choices.

Dreams from our mothers

In Reena's story, we note an important change agent – her mother. She observed that her mother was more supportive of her migration choices than her father. This – the support of older women in the family – was a consistent theme among our interviewees. In many cases, the dream of expanding choices was actively nurtured and supported by mothers, sisters and other older women in the family.

In early 2000, Ramya had an odd conversation with her PhD advisor at a US university. "My advisor had seen the films *Monsoon Wedding* and *Bend it Like Beckham*[13] in quick succession, and she was very taken with this sudden exposure to Indian culture through the movies," she remembers. Ramya's advisor noticed that, in both movies, the mothers were not as supportive of their daughters and their ambitions as the fathers. "She asked me, in these films the fathers seem more progressive and supportive while the mothers remain very traditional. 'Is this typical?'"

Ramya was taken aback by this question, since her own immigrant dreams were strongly encouraged and supported by her mother. When she discussed her advisor's observation with others, she realized that all her immigrant women friends listed their mothers as their primary support and source of inspiration. Our interviews for this book confirmed Ramya's experience. In contrast to what was shown in these two films, both significant commercial hits, the support of mothers and other, older women in the family was instrumental in empowering women to make independent migration choices. Several of the women we spoke to mentioned that they drew their inspiration primarily from their mothers, grandmothers and sisters. Only one respondent said that her father was the primary driving force behind her independent migration. The intergenerational chain of support from other women seems to be one of the dominant impetus for developing and sustaining the aspiration to break from the traditional path.

Speaking about her desire to seek out new fields of study after her bachelor's degree, Jaya remembered how much support she received from her mother. "My mother was not a BA. Still, she worked as a teacher in a municipal school. She wanted her kids to be educated." Mira also credits her mother: "My mother had encouraged my sister and me to seek economic independence, so that was always key." Kavita was more forthright about where her support came from. "My mother was 100 percent supportive; father was 0 percent supportive. He didn't want me to move alone."

Anita is one of the few women we spoke to who described their family as something other than middle class. Her family in Delhi, she said, was "affluent." She came to the US in 2005 on a company transfer. She was 25 at that time. Very focused and committed to her career, Anita reflected on the change in her family from one generation to another. "My mother is a PhD scientist, a professor. Her journey was very different from mine. She had an arranged marriage, three children. She enabled me and my sister."

The difference between Anita and her mother's path is an interesting illustration of the micropolitics of everyday life. It provides us with a glimpse of the small and subtle ways in which women assert their agency and help bring about incremental change across generations. Anita's mother's life followed the more traditional path. Anita herself is married to someone of her choice, does not have children, and has a senior position in a large consulting firm. While Anita married an American citizen, she stayed in India, working with a firm there, till she was able to find a job in the United States. She recalls that she was reluctant to move to the US to be with her husband without first finding a job that would fulfill her career aspirations.

In enabling her daughter to ask for more, to move away from the strictures of home, marriage and children, we see the assertion of Anita's mother's voice and agency. In turn, Anita is proud to say that her professional success in the US inspired her sister to also move to the States in pursuit of graduate studies and a successful career in finance. "Because of me," she said, "my sister's horizons opened up. My parents were supportive of her moving here because I came first." She also notes that she reminds her younger sister, who is single, to choose a life partner who will support her career choices. "If you are in a position to choose your husband – and for those who don't have a choice, that's a different thing – but, if you choose, be thoughtful about that choice. Think about the trade-offs first," Anita said.

This process of intergenerational transfer of aspirations and change was very well articulated in one of our most inspiring interviews. Uma is our earliest immigrant. She came to pursue a master's program at a leading science university in 1961. Uma came from a very traditional family in Mumbai. There was not a lot of emphasis on higher education in her business-oriented family. However, Uma's unusual interest in science and higher education was supported by her grandmothers. "I was the first girl in the family in four generations, so I was celebrated, which is unusual for a girl. I had an unusual situation in that my grandmother really supported my education." Uma added, "These were amazing women, my grandmothers; I think they were more adventurous than their life allowed them." She spoke of her active interest in furthering the example set by her inspiring grandmothers. When she received a monetary award from the US government for being a pioneering woman scientist, she gave gifts from that award to women across generations in her and her husband's families. "They were so excited and proud, and the men were, too. I told the younger girls that I stand on the shoulders of the women who came before me, and my shoulders are ready to hold you up."

Like Anita, several of the women we spoke to have also contributed to this process of incremental generational change by inspiring friends and younger family members. Padma's family is from a southern Indian city. She had already achieved considerable academic success with an MBA from a premier Indian institution. But she wanted to pursue a more dedicated area of research in the field of development studies. She arrived in the US in 1980 to pursue a master's degree and eventually completed a PhD program. She is now a faculty member at a US university. She believes that her independent migration choice and her professional success in the US have been inspirational to other women and girls in her family. "I go back to India now twice a year. I am definitely looked upon as a role model with my family in India, both in my generation and younger group."

Similarly, while Reena's journey was inspired by her strong reaction against her sister's arranged marriage, her journey has in turn expanded the options for her sister's daughter. Her sister and other siblings, she says, consider her a role model. "My sister always had respect for me and my ideas. She gives that freedom to her daughter, who is now 25. My niece is not married, she has a master's and is studying for her Indian Civil Service exams." Similarly her brother too looks up to her as someone who inspired him to "think big." Reena's mother would often say, she recalls, that her income had helped family members "upgrade their lives."

In Shobha's story, we see the full circle of intergeneration inspiration and change in our own sample of independent women migrants. Her family is from the western Indian city of Pune. She describes her family as middle class. Her older sister had already made her way to the US on her own. After completing her master's degree in engineering in India and gaining a few years of work experience, Shobha decided to follow her sister's path and pursue an advanced degree in a US university. Acknowledging the chain of support from the women in her family, she said, "My mom, in particular, encouraged me. I was also inspired by my sister."

Shobha arrived in the US in 1998. While her sister was already professionally established, Shobha's journey is no less independent. She saved up money from her few years of working after graduation in order to finance her travel to the US. She was also able to secure scholarships that helped her with her expenses at her US university. While financial motivations were an impetus, Shobha's main interest was in education. "Financial motivation was there. I did seek peace of mind, to get away from the daily struggle for electricity and all that. But, really, it was about education. I wanted to study in a technologically advanced country."

A passion for work and study

Many other women across the generations also echoed Shobha's academic curiosity and keen intellectual interest in their chosen field of study. Uma discovered her interest in science early on. "I loved science and mysteries. Science was a puzzle to be solved, and I loved mystery books the same way." When she got to know that some of the boys in her college were going to the US to study, Uma felt motivated to pursue her own interest in science in the US as well.

Long after Uma, in 1998, Deborah's journey to the US was motivated by the same interest in science. She had completed a master's in engineering from India. But Deborah knew that opportunities to continue in her field of hardware engineering in India would be limited. She saw an environment in India where most of the jobs were in information technology (IT) rather than hardware. Further, she noted that "in my college, there were eight girls and 65 boys, and I figured that the work environment would be impacted." So she left to pursue another master's in electrical and computer engineering, armed with a full scholarship from a US university.

Uma and Deborah described the combination of academic passion and the need to escape gendered restrictions that is a common experience among many of the women we spoke to. While being motivated by the need to sidestep gendered limitations in India, there is also a sense of excitement about the expanded academic and professional opportunities that await them. The migration decision, in other words, comes with high expectations of the possibilities for life and work in the US.

Mira spoke about this combination of motivations. As we described earlier, she did not want to follow the usual path of marriage immediately after graduation like her friends. But she also mentioned her keen interest in the scholarly environment in the US. She had considered going to the UK, but scholarships and opportunities for financing her own studies were more readily available in the US. She also felt the academic opportunities in the US were much better. "I came for the academic opportunity, because the programs here were more cut and dry."

Rekha also described similarly high pre-migration expectations. Rekha is one of the earliest immigrants in our cohort. She arrived in the US for a master's program in journalism in 1975. She described her family in southern India as upper middle class. Her mother had a bachelor's degree and was a housewife, but there were high expectations of education for girls in her family. Those expectations, it was felt, could only be fulfilled in the US. "US was in our heads, you had to go, and there was this idea that US schools were so amazing."

This excitement and expectation of expanded choices across the generations provides interesting possibilities for evaluating gender norms and restrictions globally. The pre-migration expectation of moving beyond the gender restrictions in India is often confronted with the post-migration reality of the continued gendered nature of life and work in the US.

Nilima's migration experience offers a perfect illustration of this contrast. Nilima had studied to be a medical doctor in India. But then she came upon the same sense of restricted professional choices for women in India. "I thought there would be a wide range of professional opportunities in the US. I had thought that I would eventually pursue being a surgeon in the US. In India, there are not a lot of girls who are surgeons." So in 2007, nearly a decade after Deborah, Nilima came to the US for post-graduate work with the same sense of professional interest and expectations of a more gender-neutral environment. But reflecting on her post-migration experiences, Nilima said, "I found out that it's not that different in the US – very few women go into surgery." We will explore this comparison of pre-migration expectation with the reality of post-migration experiences in greater detail in later chapters.

Conclusion

As we explored the motivations behind the immigration choices, we were once again drawn to reflect on the importance of moving beyond a limited range of stories about women's experiences. This group of independent women migrants does not fit into the more popular narratives of immigrant women. They do not face the desperate economic circumstances that are common in the popular discourse about immigrant women. They are privileged in their ability to choose fields of work and study that align with the economic imperatives that often drive US immigration laws. The vast majority of the women also came from the relatively privileged middle-class and upper-middle-class families in India, where opportunities and access to education were plentiful. It is therefore easy to slot their experiences as examples of relative middle-class privilege.

But as we delve deeper into these stories we see that there is much to be inspired by. While not fighting immediate economic deprivation, many of these women nonetheless engaged in a spirited effort to expand the constraints of gender that threatened to limit their working and personal lives. We see the choice of immigration itself being used as a tool to expand choices. We also see the ways in which women themselves transfer aspirations and effect change across generations.

Even though their pre-migration economic circumstances are not dire, future financial stability and economic independence is a concern that came up often in our interviews. All but three of the women we interviewed financed their immigrant journeys by themselves through a patchwork of savings, scholarships and borrowings from extended family that they reported returning soon after migration.

We also find that the level of support for and opposition to independent migration does not vary a great deal across the generations. Many of the women in the more recent cohort of immigrants, like Kavita, Ayesha and Reena, continued to face, if not outright opposition, at least skepticism about their decision to pursue independent journeys. This absence of a clear progression makes it even more important to highlight the kinds of subtle resistances and challenges that women are able to effect by their choices at the individual or micro level.

It is these micro-level resistances that can continue to inspire and expand the view of what is possible. For this group of women there is an expectation that their choice of the path less taken will lead to greatly expanded possibilities. What awaits them along this path? To what extent are their expectations realized? We continue this journey in the next chapters.

Notes

1 *Artsalt.com*. 2014. "Q&A: Chimamanda Ngozi Adichie Tackles Race from African Perspective in 'Americanah.'" March 4. http://www.artsatl.com/2014/03/qa-chimamanda-ngozi-adichie-americanah/ (accessed December 10, 2014).

2 Adichie, Chimamanda Ngozi Adichie. 2010. *That Thing Around Your Neck*. New York: Anchor; Adichie, Chimamanda Ngozi Adichie. 2014. *Americanah*. New York: Anchor.

3 Ehrenreich, Barbara, and Arlie Russell Hochschild. 2002. *Global Woman: Nannies, Maids, and Sex Workers in the New Economy*. New York: Henry Holt; Hondagneu-Sotelo, Pierrette. 2007. *Domestica: Immigrant Workers Cleaning*

and Caring in the Shadows of Affluence. Berkeley: University of California Press.

4 Hondagneu-Sotelo, Pierrette. 2003. *Gender and U.S. Immigration: Contemporary Trends.* Berkeley: University of California Press.

5 Dasgupta, Shamita Das. 1998. *A Patchwork Shawl: Chronicles of South Asian Women in America.* New Brunswick: Rutgers University Press; George, Sheba. 2005. *When Women Come First: Gender and Class in Transnational Migration.* Berkeley: University of California Press.

6 Mohanty, Chandra Talpade. 1984. "Under Western Eyes: Feminist Scholarship and Colonial Discourses." *Boundary 2* 12 (13): 333–358.

7 Kabeer, Naila. 2000. *The Power to Choose: Bangladeshi Garment Workers in London and Dhaka.* London: Verso.

8 The dollar amounts are based on purchasing power parity conversations of the rupee amounts.

9 Shukla, Rajesh. 2010. *How India Earns, Spends and Saves – Unmasking the Real India.* SAGE and New Delhi: NCAER.

10 In our interviews we did ask our responds about family income before migration. In most cases our respondents mentioned they were not able to recall income details accurately. This is a common issue in recall-based methods of collecting income information.

11 Krishna, Anirudh and Devendra Bajpai. 2015. "Layers in Globalising Society and the New Middle Class in India Trends, Distribution and Prospects." *Economic & Political Weekly* 50 (5): 69–77.

12 Vijaya, Ramya and Hema Swaminathan. 2015. "Engendering the Economic Measurement of Middle Class: Evidence from India." Presentation to the Eastern Economics Association Conference, New York, February.

13 Both *Monsoon Wedding*, released in 2001, and *Bend it Like Beckham*, released in 2003, depict transnational families of Indian origin.

3 Rising above or hitting the glass ceiling?

"The unseen, yet unbreachable barrier that keeps minorities and women from rising to the upper rungs of the corporate ladder, regardless of their qualifications or achievements." The Federal Glass Ceiling Commission used this definition to describe the issue that continues to resonate in the discussions about women and work in the United States. The commission's report in 1995 acknowledged the reality of the glass ceiling that confronts and restricts the career paths of qualified women and minorities in the US by pointing to the low number of women and minorities in top management positions.[1] In the years since, the debate has only intensified and, as we saw in Chapter 1, the numbers have been slow to change. Even as more and more qualified women have entered the labor force, the number of women in top management positions in the US continues to be small. In this chapter, we will discuss how our respondents view their career progression in the US relative to the high expectations of professional advancement that they had when departing India. The contrast between the expectation and the reality illuminates the glass ceiling debate in the US.

The glass ceiling in the US

The stubbornness of the ceiling is often attributed to the covert and invisible nature of the barriers that continue to reproduce traditional hierarchies within workplaces. In a key article that clarified the difference between the glass ceiling and other kinds of inequalities, the authors explain that the glass ceiling represents differences in workplaces that are not explained by "job-relevant" characteristics of the employee. That is, it has less to do with the qualifications of the employee and more to do with hidden and unstated rules of interaction, reflecting a pernicious kind of micropolitics. They further clarify that it represents a gender or racial inequality at higher levels of outcomes and that it also represents the inequality in the chances of advancement into higher levels.[2]

Over the years there has been an increasing understanding that the unspoken assumptions about gender and race create many layers of hidden exclusions, particularly at higher levels of workplace hierarchies. In her book, *Breaking the Bamboo Ceiling*, Jane Hyun explores the cultural assumptions that have resulted in the scarcity of Asian Americans in top management positions. This underrepresentation has occurred even though, as a group, Asian Americans tend to have strong academic qualifications and are well represented in junior positions. The perception that Asians are diligent workers rather than take-charge leaders has, according to Hyun and others, resulted in fewer opportunities for the kinds of organizational support and mentorships that are needed to break into top management positions. Wesley Yang also explored this issue in his 2011 article "Paper Tigers: What Happens to all of the Asian-American Overachievers When the Test-Taking Ends?" Describing the subtle nature of hidden barriers, Yang mentions, "it's really a matter of, like, small daily transactions that exact a toll on women and minorities; that we produce a power structure without there being sort of like an overt intention to keep women and minorities out."[3] Once again, we see how discrimination and barriers to progression are perpetuated by the micropolitics of the workplace.

While explicit biases are easier to identify and address through legislation, the unwritten exclusionary rules of daily interaction often endure due to their hidden nature. It is only by exploring the lived experiences of diverse groups that a better understanding of these everyday exclusions emerges and can then be explicitly addressed. Similar to the Asian-American professionals whom Hyun and Yang discuss, the education and work profiles of independent women immigrants from India make their experiences a useful vantage point to explore the hidden assumptions and barriers of the glass ceiling. As we saw in the previous chapters, immigration requirements necessitate a certain level of professional status. In addition, a passion for their field of work and interest in reaching beyond what was professionally possible in India was one of the motivators in the immigrant decision for our group of women. Their expectations for professional advancement therefore are quite high, making their observations and experiences very insightful.

Discrimination of assumptions

Uma's entire career has been about expanding the realm of possibilities for women in workplaces. With her grandmothers' support, Uma had pushed her family to accept what was at that time an uncommon ambition for women in India. There were, however, many more battles to come. When she came to the California Institute of Technology (Caltech) for a master's program in 1961, she became the first Indian woman to enroll in the prestigious institute. Uma was a pioneer not only among Indian women. To her recollection there were only seven other women students in the entire university when she arrived. It was only six years earlier that Caltech had awarded its first graduate degree to a woman.[4] Not till 1970, nine years after Uma arrived, did Caltech begin enrolling women as undergraduate students.

Throughout her career Uma, encountered many instances of hidden assumptions that limit the possibilities for women in the workplace. She remembers that professors would not invite her to go to professional, academic conferences. "They would ask the male students to go, but not me," she recollects.

> I asked my advisor about it, and he seemed surprised that I wanted to join them. I think he thought I wouldn't go with a bunch of boys who would drink and things like that. I said that I wanted to be asked, that it should be about my choice, not their assumption.

Interestingly, a recent first generation Indian immigrant who also attended graduate school at an institution famed for its science programs remembers being "a little surprised" when one of the few women in his cohort, a Pakistani woman, joined them for conferences. "She was very modestly dressed and very religious," he recalls, "but she came with us to all the conferences. She didn't drink with us, but she would sit with us. Eventually, we adapted to having her around. We would watch our language, drink less, that sort of thing." The power of assumptions, as well as the micropolitics of challenges to those assumptions, remains relevant to this day.

Uma continued to push the boundaries of her gender and her profession. She went on to complete a PhD and, through a series of publications, built her own area of research expertise and strengthened her professional reputation. But her encounters with the subtle unwritten rules of exclusion also continued. Much of her research and writing was the output of team collaboration, as is common in scientific research But, Uma noted that teamwork came with gendered assumptions, as well. "People would often assume that a man on my team was the primary author in published work," she recalls. "After a while, I insisted on being noted as the primary author in my work."

As more women entered her field, Uma saw the shifting yet persistent nature of what she says were the "discrimination of assumptions." Her field of research involved frequent trips away from home a lot. "People would assume that women with husbands or children would not want to go," she notes. "I reminded them that we should not assume these things. We should ask and remember how a woman takes care of her children is her business." Remembering her own experience of not being invited to academic conferences as a graduate student, Uma consciously became an advocate for women who came into the field after her.

The discrimination of assumptions is a recurring theme we encountered in our interviews. Ragini, based in the southern Indian city of Chennai, had completed her bachelor's degree in math and computer science in India. She came to the US for a master's program in 1998. Even though they were several decades apart, her experiences echoed those of Uma. Ragini questions the assumptions she feels people make about her commitment to her career. "My field does not have many women in general. I did feel that people were unfair to me particularly after I got married, as if my husband's career was naturally #1." She remembers that, soon after being married, she moved to Europe on a six-month assignment. This temporary separation from her husband, she said, led to "a lot of issues" because others were questioning her decision to accept the overseas position.

Nilima, too, mentioned having encountered the tendency to underesti- mate women's ambitions. As noted in a previous chapter, she had initially wanted to pursue a career as a surgeon. She realized, however, that fulfilling this ambition would be as difficult in the US as it had been in India. She then pursued another area of medical research, completed her graduate educa- tion and joined a large consulting firm. Despite the fact that it has a diverse workforce, she feels that the firm does have an "all-boys club," and being included in this club helps professional development.

She quickly realized that she had to assert her ambitions much more actively than she was accustomed to.

> I was not fully aware about how I should negotiate the job and my level. I could have done better initially, but I learnt quickly to be more aggressive. I feel that, for men, promotions are based on potential while women have to prove themselves.

Attempting to be more assertive also created another set of assumptions. Nilima said, "I also think women are seen as bitches if they are aggressive or argumentative, and that is not the case for men."

Being meek, being Indian

Treading the fine line between assertiveness and argumentativeness seems to be particularly fraught for Indian women, given the combination of gen- der and racial expectations. Anita articulated the dilemma for Indian women quite bluntly. "Indian women are bred to be meek, to be good listeners." Anita has an MBA from a prestigious Indian institution. She moved to the US from the Indian office of a large technology multinational corporation through an inter-company transfer. In the US office, the perception of being meek proved to be a liability. "It was a very American work environment. It was hard for me to find my own voice; it's like I almost wasn't there." Finding that voice or at least the right pitch is not easy, particularly when the expectation is that Indian women will be meek. Vani, a software engineer, describes her challenge as an Indian woman. "There is gender bias everywhere, in India, the US, everywhere, and it comes out in different ways. Here, some women are tolerated more if they are ambitious and soft spoken." Vani arrived in 1998 through the extended stay work visa for specialty occupations (H-1B) when she was recruited by a US based company. In her field of software engineering, Vani recalled, many people were moving abroad from India. It seemed to her that migration was the natural choice for professional advancement. But once here, being a woman and particularly being an Indian woman brought a confusing set of assumptions and expectations. "I have swung on the pendulum from being assertive to putting myself in the background. I am sorry to say that I have not found the ideal middle ground."

Shobha and Reena's experiences more directly describe the dilemma of finding a voice amidst a combined gendered and racial expectation of meekness. Shobha described a tough situation she once faced at work. "I was unable to say 'no' to a very demanding situation, where there were high expectations and very limited resources." She noticed that her manager, a woman, ignored her while paying attention to a junior person who was not Indian.

> It was body language, not verbal. This is a common problem among Indians and Asians, not wanting to say no, not asking for help, not pushing back. I was scared initially and then got fed up and went to HR. I told them I would quit if things did not change.

Reena found that learning to push back had its own risks. Reena had often been told that she was too meek, too quiet in the workplace. She then decided to become more assertive about issues that concerned her work environment.

> In one job, we had been going back and forth on salary negotiations. When I asked for a raise that we had earlier discussed, my white male supervisor was angry. It became a nasty and political exchange with him and HR.

With the matter escalating, Reena lodged a formal complaint with the civil liberties office. She later learned from the mediators that her boss had complained that she was too quiet and had a lot of language and cultural issues that made her a bad fit at work. Ironically, the complaint about her being too quiet only surfaced after she had irked her boss by speaking up and asking for a raise.

One among a few: the policy context of women in STEM

The confusion about the gendered expectations regarding assertiveness is heightened for Indian immigrant women, since, in many cases, they work in fields where there are few women. Even for more recent cohorts, the work environment is, in some ways, not very different from the one Uma encountered decades ago. Ragini and Vani, both software engineers, stressed that there were few women in their field, whether in India or the US. Vani noted that, in her most recent project, there were only about five women in a team of 125. Deborah, who migrated hoping for better opportunities in her field of hardware engineering, joined a large multinational corporation after completing her master's program. She pointed out that, while her company is usually known for being a diverse and international workplace, she was the only person from a minority group in her team.

The common thread here is that Uma, Ragini, Vani, Deborah and, in fact, a majority of the women we spoke to have a background in science and technology related fields (STEM) of work and study. This pattern is consistent across the generations. In each post-1965 decade, we were able to identify relatively fewer women in other fields. This is not unexpected, since it mirrors the overall trend and perception of Indian immigrants in the US. Neither is this trend accidental or an indication of a natural affinity for STEM among Indian women. It is in fact a product of specific governmental policies in both countries.

There is a long history of prioritizing science and technology related fields in India's education policy. India's first prime minister, Jawaharlal Nehru, had a vision of harnessing science and science education to address the substantial economic development challenge that the country faced at the time of independence in 1947. His strong belief in this vision led to the adoption of the Science Policy Resolution by the government of India in 1958. A landmark policy that was the first of its kind for a developing economy, the resolution specifically linked science, science education and the role of the welfare state in improving the living standards of its citizens. As part of this effort, the government supported the development of a high profile network of state institutions of research and higher education in science and technology.[5]

State policy valorized science as worth studying in the interest of the nation. It also signaled the availability of jobs in a sector that the state was helping expand. As a result, a strong culture of preference for studying science has taken root, since that stream can help those who are aspiring for financially stable professions.[6] This preference continues to be so strong that choosing to study social science or humanities tends to be considered a sign of academic failure. For women, studying science helps signal their intent to seriously pursue a career. The authors of this book recall being questioned about their choice to study social science in high school even though they were "good students." Padma recalls that, when she got into a prestigious institution for an MBA program, she "could not tell my middle-class family that I would turn down [the opportunity] . . . [But] I never really enjoyed the coursework."

This policy-driven culture of science education in India coincided with the restructuring of immigration policies in the US in the 1960s to create an immigration pathway for Indian STEM professionals. The 1965 restructuring of policies in the US specifically prioritized immigrants with skills that are in short supply in the US. Even today, primary immigrants who want to become permanent residents have to show that their skills are required and useful to the US economy. The most consistently valued skills in the US have been those held by STEM professionals.

The temporary extended stay work visa categories that are often the stepping-stone for permanent migration are good indicators of this preference for STEM professionals. The largest category of such temporary extended stay visas is the H1-B or the "specialty occupations" category for high-skilled immigrants. In 2012, a majority (64 percent) of the H-1B visa holders were from India. Within the H-1B category, a majority of the visas are issued in the STEM fields. Figure 3.1 provides information on

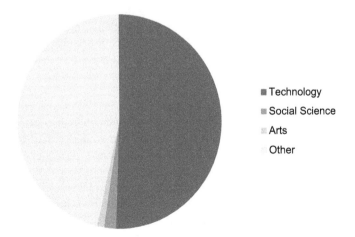

■ Technology
▨ Social Science
▧ Arts
   Other

Figure 3.1 Occupations receiving H-1B visas (2012)

categories that H-1B visas are given to. Even within the STEM field, there is a very narrow range of occupations that get priority. As Figure 3.1 shows, 50 percent of the H-1B visas were issued only for computer-related occupations (Department of Homeland Security 2013). Occupations that are not STEM related make up a very minuscule portion of the H-1B visas. For example, only 1.9 percent of the H-1B visas were issued for social science occupations. Arts-related occupations received an even smaller portion, 1.1 percent of the visas.[7]

Given this selection bias, it is perhaps to be expected that the immigrant dreams of women are more likely to be realized if they are in the STEM fields that are considered most useful to the US economy. Discussing this feature of immigration laws, Prashad has eloquently stated that immigrants are, after all, wanted "for their labor and not for their lives."[8] Independent and motivated women in non-STEM fields of work and study who might also want to use migration as a way to expand their life choices might get fewer opportunities to do so.

Though the concentration of Indian immigrant women in STEM fields, even if it is the outcome of policy bias, is distinctive, given the overall gender trends in STEM in the US. According to a U.S. Department of Commerce study, while women hold nearly half of the jobs in the US, they fill only 25 percent of the jobs in the STEM fields. This relatively small representation of women in STEM has generated a lot of popular and policy attention.[9] For example, the Office of Science and Technology Policy, in collaboration with the White House Council on Women and Girls, has a stated mission to increase "the participation of women and girls – as well as other underrepresented groups – in the fields of science, technology, engineering, and mathematics."[10] In adopting this mission the Council has emphasized the importance of women's participation as a way to ensure a sizeable and growing STEM workforce in the US. It has also pointed out that increasing participating in STEM is important from the perspective of greater economic equality for women, given the potential for high incomes in these fields.

Parallel to the policy focus, the "women in STEM" issue has also attracted a lot of popular attention in the media and public discourse. This discourse has focused on the barriers that prevent women from not only entering STEM fields but also from reaching the higher levels in STEM-related workplaces. This discussion has often been controversial. For example, in 2005, Larry Summers, then-President of Harvard University, created intense backlash when his comments at a public talk seemed to suggest that there needs to be an investigation of whether innate gender differences in ability and motivation account for the lack of women in higher levels of STEM professions. His comments continue to resonate as many others have since countered that it is in fact the gender stereotyping and the lack of support and mentoring at workplaces that is the main problem for women in STEM.[11]

The experiences of Indian immigrant women who have already experienced gendered limitations in another context provide a useful perspective to this debate. Their level of motivation is high since in many cases they made migration decisions based on their interest in advancing to higher levels in their STEM careers. Yet the assumptions and attitudes they encounter in the US reminds them that migration did not solve all their gender concerns. The battle for access and progress continues, albeit in a different form.

One of the interesting dynamics we found in some of our interviews is the encounter between Indian immigrant women and another particularly big immigrant group in STEM fields- Indian men. Here we found that gender issues seem to overlay and at times override commonalities in racial experiences. Padma, an electrical engineer, commented on Indian's men's ability to integrate more easily with the unwritten rules of workplace interactions. "I feel that Indian men solve that problem quicker because they talk about sports more easily." Kavita, a human resources professional shared her observations about the advantage Indian men have in the meekness versus assertiveness debate. "The main issue I find is Indian men versus Indian women. Indian men have projected themselves as geeky while Indian women are meek in comparison."

With the possibility of easier integration, Indian men seem to align their interests more along gender lines and offer limited support to Indian women. Shobha recalls a time with a difficult male boss, who was from a European country. "He would shout at me, take my keyboard etc. and I felt it was because I was an Indian woman . . . I was scared to complain because of my H-1 visa." Finally, Shobha told her boss's boss who was Indian. But Shobha said, "He didn't do anything." Elaborating further on her encounter with the assumption that she might not be serious about her career, Ragini mentioned, "Indian men's comments were particularly obnoxious." She felt that other Indian men in her male-dominated field assumed that her husband's career would be top priority.

This global nature of gendered interactions among Indian professionals is perhaps reflected in yet another STEM controversy. Almost a decade after Larry Summers, a statement by an Indian immigrant man drew heated attention once again to the debate about the barriers for women in STEM. In 2014, at a public forum organized specifically to discuss some of these barriers, Satya Nadella the Chief Executive Officer of Microsoft was asked what advice he would give to women who tend to be uncomfortable asking for raises. This lack of assertiveness in salary negotiations is often cited as one of the causes for the persistent gender pay gap in STEM fields.[12] As we have seen in our interviews, women often feel that striking the right tone in assertiveness is difficult given the gendered ideas about being assertive versus being aggressive or argumentative.

Nadella, a first generation Indian immigrant, replied,

> It's not about asking for the raise but knowing and having faith that the system will actually give you the right raises as you go along . . . And that, I think, might be one of the additional superpowers that quite frankly women who don't ask for a raise have. Because that's good karma. It'll come back because somebody's going to know "that's the kind of person that I want to trust."[13]

In implying that women should not try to be assertive but just trust the system, Nadella's response seemed to indicate a lack of awareness about the barriers of assumptions and attitudes that women in STEM encounter.

In a quick and heated backlash, many pointed out to Nadella that the system in fact routinely fails to reward women as much as it does men, which is why the debate exists in the first place. To his credit, Nadella responded to the backlash by acknowledging that he was wrong and that his advice "underestimated exclusion and bias – conscious and unconscious – that can hold people back."[14] As we have seen here, race and gender combine to form a complex set of conscious and unconscious exclusions that Indian women have to learn to navigate.

Proving their worth in the non-STEM fields

For Indian immigrant women in non-STEM fields, the assumptions and exclusions they encounter are equally complex. Aligning their choice of work and study with the instrumental nature of immigration policies is often their first challenge. Outside of the STEM fields, proving that they can make a valuable contribution to the United States is often a difficult process even for immigrant women with advanced degrees. Their journeys therefore tend to be more complicated and involve multiple attempts.

Rekha went back to India after completing her master's program in India because she found it challenging to find a suitable job in the US. She returned after a few years to complete her PhD and eventually established an academic career. Asha, a language and cultural studies student, first had stopovers in Europe, where she was able to secure scholarships to complete advanced degrees, before she made her way to the US. Similarly Reena, also in language studies, traveled to another country for graduate study before arriving in the US.

There have been times when the instrumental nature of the immigrant laws has opened opportunities for specific groups of non-STEM women. A severe shortage of nurses in the US in the 1970s and 80s led to nursing being considered a priority occupational category for immigrants. One of the earliest immigrants in our interview cohort, Maryam, was recruited to fill this need for nurses in 1970. Just 20 years old at the time, Maryam was encouraged by her family to respond to an advertisement from a hospital in Pennsylvania.

But the inclusion of nursing in the list of priority occupations for immigration has not been permanent. Maryam's generation of immigrant nurses helped the US address a severe shortage in the 1970s. Once the shortage was less severe, there were fewer opportunities for immigrant nurses. The 1990s brought another wave of shortages. In response to this, a new temporary extended stay visa category for nurses was introduced in 1999. However, in 2009 this visa category was terminated – once again narrowing the range of opportunities for women in non-STEM fields.[15]

Immigrants in STEM fields are viewed as bringing in skills that make them valuable, even indispensable, to the US economy. In contrast, those in non-STEM fields can encounter more overt manifestations of racial and gender stereotyping. Rekha had returned to India after her master's in the US and had established an impressive professional record there. She then returned to the US in the 1980s to pursue a PhD in a humanities discipline. Rekha remembers being told by her graduate school advisor that international students were not given teaching assistantships in their first semester, presumably because of concerns about their ability to communicate in English. She persisted and eventually got a teaching assistantship in the English department teaching remedial English. But even here, she remembers, "The students would look at me as if to say, 'Who are you to teach me English?'"

After her PhD, when Rekha began an academic career as a faculty member, she continued to encounter doubts about her work. She recalled,

> My initial years in the field were difficult. I used to do a lot of India-related work, and I was asked to "broaden" my area of study. I was the only person of color doing postcolonial work, and it wasn't welcome.

Rekha's interest in studying non-white cultures was questioned since her chosen field was, at the time, "parochial and Eurocentric." She eventually went on to establish herself as a respected and pioneering scholar. In her story, too, we see the micropolitics of challenging traditional boundaries in gender and race in the workplace.

Rekha's experience of encountering a racial glass ceiling at higher levels in the academy is echoed by Padma. Padma completed a PhD in a social science discipline in the US in 1991 and became a faculty member at a large research university. Padma mentioned, "Our institutions in the US are still male dominated, especially at the higher levels, and they are still racist." In her university, Padma mentioned, there were many women administrators and an active feminist scholarly cohort. Nonetheless, she notes that there are very few faculty of color who are full professors. Despite her own personal success, Padma believes that many academic institutions in the US are male dominated and continue to have racial biases.

Conclusion

As we follow the post-immigrant lives of our cohort, we see the interactions between the micro struggles of individuals and the macropolitics and policies of the global political economy. These intersections make immigrant narratives insightful on many dimensions. At the macro level, a combination of education and immigration policy biases in both India and the US has created opportunities for some groups of women while excluding others.

In the stories of these relatively privileged and professional group of women immigrants, we uncover nuanced and hidden details about the interactions of race and gender in workplaces. As we continue to follow their journeys, we see that the women are not mere observers of the constraints that they confront. Their immigration choices are centered round pushing boundaries and finding ways to expand possibilities pre- and post-migration. In many cases the very presence of these women in fields effects change. Many of our respondents, including Uma, Padma and Radha, personify such change in themselves and their professions. As new boundaries appear post-migration, many view it a continuation of that journey. Reflecting on not just her own journey but also on what she advises other women in her capacity as a senior executive in her organization, Anita mentioned, "I don't want women to step back with their sob stories – let's talk about constructive solutions." In the next chapter we explore the way and the extent to which immigrant women have joined the conversation about finding constructive solutions to the constraints they continue to encounter.

Notes

1 Federal Glass Ceiling Commission. 1995. *A Solid Investment: Making Full Use of the Nation's Human Capital.* http://www.dol.gov/dol/aboutdol/history/reich/reports/ceiling2.pdf (accessed December 1, 2014).
2 Cotter, David A., Joan M. Hermsen, Seth Ovadia, and Reeve Vanneman. 2001. "The Glass Ceiling Effect." *Social Forces* 80 (2): 655–681.

3 Hyun, Jane. 2005. *Breaking the Bamboo Ceiling*. New York: Harper Collins; National Public Radio. 2014. "Does the 'Bamboo Ceiling' Shut Asian Americans Out of Top Jobs?" May 23. http://www.npr.org/2014/05/23/315129852/does-a-bamboo-ceiling-shut-asian-americans-out-of-top-jobs (accessed December 5, 2014); Yang, Wesley. 2011. "Paper Tigers: What Happens to All the Asian-American Overachievers When the Test-Taking Ends?" *New York Magazine*, May 3. http://nymag.com/news/features/asian-americans-2011–5/ (accessed December 7, 2014).

4 In 1955, Dorothy Ann Semenow received a PhD in chemistry and biology. Caltech Archives. 2013. "Facts about Caltech History." http://archives.caltech.edu/about/fastfacts.html (accessed December 5, 2014).

5 Institutions within this network such as the various Indian Institutes of Technologies are widely regarded as among the best in the world. For more information, please see Indian National Science Academy. 2001. *Pursuit and Promotion of Science: The Indian Experience*. New Delhi: INSA.

6 Prashad, Vijay. 2001. *The Karma of Brown Folk*. Minneapolis, MN: University of Minnesota Press..

7 Department of Homeland Security. 2013. "Characteristics of H1-B Specialty Occupation Workers, Fiscal Year 2012 Annual Report to Congress." http://www.uscis.gov/sites/default/files/USCIS/Resources/Reports%20and%20Studies/H-1B/h1b-fy-12-characteristics.pdf (accessed December 20, 2014).

8 Prashad 2001, p. 76.

9 Department of Commerce. 2011. "Women in STEM: A Gender Gap to Innovation." http://www.esa.doc.gov/sites/default/files/womeninstemagaptoinnovation8311.pdf (accessed December 15, 2014).

10 More information is available at https://www.whitehouse.gov/administration/eop/ostp/women.

11 Eileen, Pollack. 2013. "Why Are There Still So Few Women in Science?" *New York Times*, October 3. http://www.nytimes.com/2013/10/06/magazine/why-are-there-still-so-few-women-in-science.html?pagewanted=all&_r=0 (accessed December 21, 2014); Urry, Meg. 2005. "Diminished by Discrimination We Scarcely See." *Washington Post*, February 6. http://www.washingtonpost.com/wp-dyn/articles/A360–2005Feb5.html (accessed December 22, 2014).

12 By some estimates, a 14 % gender wage gap persists in STEM fields: For every dollar earned by a man in STEM, a woman earns 14 cents less. (U.S. Department of Commerce, 2011)

13 *Washington Post*. 2014. "Microsoft CEO's Remarks about Raises Shouldn't Just Be Unsettling to Women." October 10. http://www.washingtonpost.com/blogs/on-leadership/wp/2014/10/10/microsoft-ceos-remarks-about-raises-shouldnt-just-be-unsettling-to-women/ (accessed December 26, 2014).

14 *GeekWire*. 2014. "Internal Memo: Microsoft CEO Satya Nadella Sets New Diversity Plan after 'Humbling' Experience." October 15. http://www.geekwire.com/2014/internal-memo-microsoft-ceo-sets-new-diversity-plan-humbling-experience/ (accessed December 27, 2014).

15 Sheba George, herself the daughter of an immigrant nurse, documents the experiences of women in nursing in her book, *When Women Come First* (2005).

4   Leaning in and reaching out

Personal networks and political processes

In our interviews, when we asked women to reflect on how they navigated their way through the American workplace, many of them mentioned Sheryl Sandberg's best-selling book, *Lean In: Women, Work, and the Will to Lead.*[1] In her book Sandberg exhorts women to "take a seat at the table" and to proactively seek out mentors, allies and professional opportunities. She notes that men tend to be significantly more adept at building social capital – relationships based on reciprocity that are key to success in the workplace. While acknowledging barriers that women may face, she regularly exhorts women to take ownership of this challenge and proactively seek out sponsors who can help them navigate their careers.[2] In this chapter, we see that our respondents have developed creative ways to develop their careers through professional and personal ties. In some ways, Indian immigrant women have long been following Sandberg's playbook. However, we will see that public policies and collective action have also been crucial to their success. The experiences we describe below show us that professional advancement is certainly helped by individual strategies that can nudge changes in assumptions and attitudes. At the same, larger organization and structural changes are required to dismantle the gender and racial barriers that continue to exist.

The debate over *lean in*

Given her standing as one of the few successful women at the top of the hierarchy in the technology industry, Sandberg's work has attracted a lot of attention. It provided a new spotlight to the ongoing discussion about women and the glass ceilings they encounter. Her exhortations to be proactive about seeking and seizing professional opportunities inspired many women. At the same time, her arguments are controversial because they put the onus of breaking the ceiling on women themselves. In a prominent critique of Sandberg's work, Faludi notes that Sandberg undervalues the fact that women are often constrained by the gender-unfriendly work environment that they encounter. By asking women to shoulder the responsibility to "lean in," Faludi argues, Sandberg is narrowing her focus to elite women who are well-placed to develop and implement individual networking strategies.[3] For women whose socio-economic status or other vulnerabilities make it harder to push back in workplaces, such tactics are less useful than policy-based measures.

The experiences of Indian immigrant women offer an interesting perspective to this larger debate about individual strategies versus collective and policy action against the gender and race ceilings at workplaces. Many of our interviewees feel that they should heed Sandberg's advice and take individual responsibility for building social capital. As we noted in the previous chapter, Anita was forthright about finding "constructive solutions" rather than recounting "sob stories." As one of our respondents also reminded us, the middle-class professional status of Indian immigrant women and their fluency with English ensures that their circumstances in the US usually represent a more privileged status than those women of color who come from deprived socio-economic backgrounds. Many of our respondents feel, therefore, empowered to implement Sandberg's exhortations to proactively build networks.

At the same time, the stories we recount also highlight the limitations of such an individualized strategy. We see that race, gender and immigration status create unique vulnerabilities that make it difficult to fully operationalize Sandberg's networking advice. One of our acquaintances noted that her professional status as a senior executive in a large company enables her to access mentors and networks that are usually unavailable to more disadvantaged groups of immigrants. But she also shared her dilemma about putting Sandberg's suggestion into action. "You know what?" she exclaimed.

> No one invites me to their golf meetings. I am single and I am an Indian woman. I just don't get those calls. And if I try to step forward, people will think I am too aggressive or a flirt.

The early immigrants: crossing ethnic and gender boundaries

The importance of social capital has been emphasized in academic work long before Sandberg's book made it a talking point. In his famous work on social networks, Robert Putnam describes the importance of systems of trust, norms and behavioral expectations that can result in social coordination and mutual benefit.[4] Since then many social scientists have underscored the importance of strong social capital in attaining upward mobility in the workplace.[5]

As outsiders, immigrants traditionally have access to fewer networks and have to build from scratch. To make up for this deficit, they have often relied on shared ethnicity and intersecting economic interests as sources of social capital. Members of one subsection of the Indian Gujarati community, who own and operate several motels across the US, form one such closely knit, mutually supportive ethnic social and economic enclave. Family linkages are the bedrock of such networks. Mitra shows us another example of social networking based on ethnic ties among the Indian-Punjabi taxi drivers in New York. Taxi drivers from India – and, in particular, the state of Punjab – establish a close and dependable network of trust, based on family links, common or neighboring residences, common religion, shared dining habits and mutually provided financial help. The mobilization of social capital within this group helps them find and sustain their niche in the taxi industry in New York.[6]

In contrast, the workplaces of our respondents are not based on co-ethnic ties. The women, therefore, have limited recourse to the advantages and comforts of ethnic bonding that immigrant groups have traditionally relied upon. While some of the more recent immigrants we interviewed had siblings, cousins, uncles or aunts already based in the US, such family connections do not provide the kind of direct social capital that Gujarati motel owners and the Punjabi taxi drivers could take advantage of. How, then, do these women build their professional support groups?

Earlier groups of women immigrants were particularly isolated since they did not have family connections or pre-existing networks of Indian migrants. In 1961, when Uma arrived at Caltech, there were few women there, and no Indian women at all. Similarly, when Jaya arrived in 1973 on a student visa, there were very few single Indian women in the city. Maryam came to the US in 1970 when she was recruited for a nursing job in a hospital. Although it was a time when several foreign nurses were recruited to fill a nursing shortage, she was still the only Indian nurse at her hospital and did not meet any other single Indian women. She reports feeling very lonely and wanting to go home.

Lacking the traditional immigrant route of ethnic bonding, Uma, Jaya and Maryam's generation had to build networks not just at work but also in their personal lives as well. This they did with *chutzpah* and spirited determination. After completing her master's degree Jaya was unable to find work in the city where she had first arrived in the US. So she decided to try her luck in another city.

> I needed to find an internship, so I took a bus to Atlanta, where I stayed with a friend. I opened up a phone book and started calling doctors that I could work with. One doctor asked me if I was Indian.

I guess he figured that out from my name. He said that he had had good experiences in working with Indians before and called me for an interview. . . . I went and got the job! While standing at the bus stop heading back, I was wondering where I would stay in Atlanta. I then met another Indian family also waiting for their bus. We struck up a conversation and they offered me a place to stay while I looked for an apartment. And, that was it, that's how I got to Atlanta.

Her internship led to a long and fruitful working relationship with the doctor who first employed her.

With no in-group Indian affiliate community to reach out to, Uma relied on friendships with other women. She remembers,

I was an anomaly but people were good to me. I had a few other women friends. They were not Indian, but they were my roommates and my friends. They helped me learn to do housework and get adjusted to life in the US. They also understood my lifestyle. They would tell me in advance when they were cooking non-vegetarian food, and I would stay out of the apartment till they were done.

Uma showed a great deal of determination to make a space for herself in her professional world as well. She directly questioned her professors' tendency to invite only male graduate students to attend conferences. Later on in her professional career, she also challenged assumptions that might restrict opportunities for younger women scientists. Uma herself notes her faith in networking and building social capital a la Sandberg:

I believe strongly in networks and maintaining your networks. I have had great women mentors. The principal of my school in India told us that we should not hold ourselves back as women, and I believed her. She was progressive and inspiring.

But as we follow Uma's story we also realize that, while her own efforts on behalf of herself and her junior colleagues are inspiring, her career was also helped by government initiatives to expand opportunities for women. After her PhD, Uma secured a federal research grant. Soon after, she got a permanent position at a federal government scientific research organization. It was here that she built her area of expertise and had her own research team. Uma reflected, "The federal government was ahead of the private sector in hiring women scientists." Beyond hiring, Uma also noted that the government has played an important role in equalizing opportunities in later stages as well. As more women scientists started joining the organization

Uma mentioned that "DC [as the seat of federal government] wanted to see more gender equity" in opportunities within the organization as well. Jaya's career also involved help from policy intended to expand the field. After her adventurous start in Atlanta, Jaya moved to another state to work and secured a government grant to work on a laboratory geared towards minorities. Eventually, Jaya used her experience and determination to set up her own lab.

Maryam's experience at work was different from the other early immigrants since her area of expertise, nursing, is traditionally considered the purview of women. In fact, Maryam mentioned feeling quite confident about her work when she first came to the US.

> Work-wise we knew more. Nursing training in India was more intense. I knew how to start an IV line, which many graduate nurses here didn't know. Here everything needs a certification. In India the training was more comprehensive, and you knew a lot without having to wait for individual certifications.

She was able to complete her US certifications and licenses fairly quickly. The hospital where she was first hired paid for her certifications.

She felt less confident about building a life in the US in the initial years. The gender and ethnicity barriers were more acutely felt in her life outside of work. "I was so lonely initially. . . . I was the only Indian. Other nurses were friendly, they used to ask me out, but I was not used to that culture of going out at night." Interestingly, Jaya recalls the same sense of discomfort about joining her colleagues for "late night trips to bars." Things changed gradually for Maryam. As periodic nursing shortages continued in the US in the 1970s and 80s, eventually, more nurses were recruited from India as well. Once established with their US certifications, the nurses were able to sponsor immediate family members on the family visa category. Maryam herself sponsored her brother and his family. Sheba George's book documents similar stories of family sponsorship by women nurses. Together with their extended families, Indian nurses cultivated a tightly knit community in the US.[7]

In keeping with the pioneering spirit that led her to become an early independent woman migrant, Maryam went back to college and pursued a master's degree in health administration. As she transitioned to a position in nursing administration, Maryam recalled that she also made a gradual transition in her outlook about socializing after work. "Now I have to go for certain kind of gatherings, since I joined an administrative position. Slowly I did get acclimated and changed my attitude a bit." A combination of policy imperatives that led to more international nursing recruitment and allowed family visa sponsorship and her own personal fortitude helped Maryam in eventually forming a personal and social network in the US.

Changes in the networking space

Women who arrived in later decades were able to take advantage of increasingly sophisticated networks that had been created, in part, by previous waves of immigrants. Over the years these networks have provided an important counterpoint to the barriers of ethnicity and gender that the early immigrants encountered in the initial stages of their journey. Rekha, who arrived in the US as a student in 1975 and is now a professor, observed, "These days, I see Indian students being picked up by other students at the airport, being housed by them. We did not have any of those things when I arrived."[8] Padma arrived at a large research university some years after Rekha. She recalls being confused about how to send a telegram to her parents and encountering another Indian woman at the post office who became her friend early on. While Padma benefited from a large South Asian community in her university, she also recalls feeling out of sorts with the systems in the US. Another respondent recalls being baffled by how to use an ATM and asking another international student for help.

It is unlikely that a more recent student arrival would encounter similar challenges to adjusting to life in the US. As she was preparing to arrive as a student in 1999, Biswas received a detailed email with information on what to bring and not to bring to the United States. "Don't bother bringing a coat to Chicago just to save dollars," noted the email. "You will not find anything in India that will prepare you for Chicago winters. When you get here, we will tell you about the stores where you can get discounted winter coats." "Do bring a large pressure cooker," the note added. "Your roommates and you will often cook your meals together." Bidisha had a friend in Chicago with whom she stayed for a few days immediately after her arrival. Her eventual roommate, also a newly arrived student, was housed by other Indian students. Both Biswas and her roommate were able to glean valuable information from the Indian student network on how best to adjust to their university and their adopted city.

The transition from study to work

Student networks have come a long way and have provided substantial support to recent cohorts of immigrants. Yet such networks have not been as easily replicated in the working world outside the universities. Many universities actively provide support for student networks, making their services effective and stable. On the other hand, workplace networks, at least for Indian immigrant women, seem to be less consistent in their usefulness.

Shobha's story provides us with interesting insights into the difference between universities and the workplace in terms of establishing immigrant social networks that are supportive of women. Shobha arrived in 1999 on a student (F-1) visa. Her earliest mentor in the country was her older sister, who had come to the US a few years earlier. The sister provided her with an abundance of information on cultural and work practices in the US. After settling into her university, she was able to tap into pre-existing networks to build her skill and knowledge base. "My university had a very well-developed program to help international students," she recounted.

> In the process, I was able to make friends with other Indians, with Chinese students and other international students. It was so comfortable that I didn't even realize I was living in a rural part of the country. . . . I was also active with the South Asian student organization. In my second year, I became an advisor for incoming international students. That was my way of giving back. I also had an American host family. They taught me to drive, they provided me with insights into regular American life.

Shobha, as well as some of our other respondents who arrived as students, also recalled that other Indian students provided her with valuable information on how to write resumes and how to present herself at job interviews.

After completing her studies, Shobha got a job with a large American corporation based in the Midwest. Here, she encountered initial professional challenges in the US.

> When I moved to a new city for a job, I consciously decided to live alone and not have a roommate so that I could have independence and flexibility. . . . At work, though, I think that being an Indian woman did make some things difficult. I had problems with my first boss, and I felt that some of his behavior towards me was because I am Indian. I was too scared, though, to complain. It was because of visa, the H-1.

Shobha's fears regarding her visa status are a common refrain among immigrants in general and often constrains them from speaking out in difficult professional situations.

Shobha's challenges continued to grow.

> Then I got laid-off. I had a month before my visa status would expire. It was a stressful time, because I had put so much into being on my own and now I didn't have a job. It was emotionally traumatic. In the end, I got a different job in the same company in three weeks. That job was much more suited to me, as it was more cross-functional, diverse and more people-oriented.

In the absence of the supportive immigrant networks that have developed among students over the years, the vulnerabilities of being an immigrant and being "different" seems to get accentuated in the workplace. For women without access to the supportive university networks that Shobha had initially, finding their voice has been harder still. Anita, Vani and Puja were all fairly successful in their careers in India. Wanting to avoid the stagnation that often confronts mid-career women, they choose to explore new avenues in the US. Post-migration, all the professional women we interviewed reported receiving very little support for their transition. When asked if she had joined any groups that might have helped her settle in, Vani, who moved to the US on a work visa asked, "Are there any organizations that reach out to women like me? If so, I would love to hear about them."

Accepting the networking challenge

Yet like the early immigrants, each successive cohort of women has found creative ways to both acclimatize and to effect their own micropolitics of change. When confronted with this challenge of finding a voice at work, we found that Sandberg's call to be proactive resonated with many of the women. Shobha personifies someone who has been able to learn and apply interpersonal skills in support of her social capital and mobility.

During my lay-off period, I realized that networks are the most important thing. I became active in my company's women's groups and a group that reached out to other Asians in the organization. I also joined a group for young professionals in the city.

These groups proved to be invaluable to Shobha's career.

Joining these groups made me more self-aware. For example, we would talk about how Asians often smile a lot and have difficulty saying no. Once you are aware of these characteristics, you realize that they can be misunderstood, and then you can neutralize the negative effect.

Other than the cultural impact, joining the group also enabled Shobha to become

more aware of organizational politics and structure. These associations helped me build ties to peers and also those who were one or two levels above me. My mobility within the company was eased by my association with these groups. . . . In the end, the layoff was the best thing that could happen to me. At the time, though, it felt just awful.

Reflecting on what her networks taught her, Shobha asserted that "Indian women often miss out on the importance of networking, self-promotion, building our brand. These groups that I joined helped me understand the importance of those things in the American work culture."

Like Shobha, Deborah taught herself to be more self-aware about behavioral traits that a predominantly white group of colleagues might find unusual. She reflected, "In the beginning, the challenge was just not knowing. You think that, if you work hard you will be successful. Then you realize that working hard is a given, you have to network." Deborah now works in a team that is very diverse and has found that diversity to be comforting and rewarding. Here, she has been able to join support groups that helped her with networking. "I joined diversity groups; that was helpful because in a big company, you don't know where to go for networking."

The limits of individual networking efforts

Puja moved to the United States after considerable work experience in India. Now a consultant, she reflected on a particular barrier that she faced in her new professional environment:

> I can make small talk, but my context is different. I can't really do the sports talk thing. The only topic I have left, then, to chat about is my child, so I make conversation about that with people who have children.

The issue of "talking sports" was a very common refrain among our respondents. Even Shobha, with her initial years of cultural immersion in the university system, noted that her lack of interest in American sports continues to be an impediment to workplace socializing. Puja commented on the gendered aspect of sports talk. "I feel that Indian men solve that problem quicker because they talk about sports more easily." One other gendered and cultural impediment to networking recurred in our conversations. Maryam and Jaya's discomfort with the "culture of going out at night" continued to be echoed by later generations of women. Decades after Maryam, Shobha mentioned, "I don't drink much; that's a big part of work-based socialization in the US. I feel like I have missed out on networking because of that, because of my lack of interest in happy hours."

Besides these cultural issues, a big obstacle to the individual effort to find a voice at work is the ever-present fear, at least in the initial years, about visa status. Despite the considerable inroads Shobha made towards building her social capital after her first experience of being laid off, the networks she managed to cultivate have not provided consistent protection against race and gender issues in the workplace. This is particularly the case when employees feel vulnerable due to their visa status. After her initial job switch, Shobha found herself in a more supportive environment. Some time later, however, she had to work under a manager who had "a racist attitude." Shobha felt that this manager's body language and overall demeanor demonstrated a preference for other, white employees in the team. Confronted with this situation, Shobha found her old fears coming back. "I was worried about the ramifications, especially because my green card was in process at the time." Eventually she did decide to speak up – not a decision that many are able to make.

Many, if not most, of the women we interviewed have consciously sought out workplaces with high levels of diversity as a way of navigating around cultural and ethnic barriers. The cultural and visa barriers that hamper their visibility in very American work environments seems to matter less when they are able to interact with a diverse workforce. Anita, who had felt invisible after an inter-company transfer to the US, followed this route. "Even though I was qualified, it was difficult. So, I left because I needed a more diverse workforce." She subsequently found her groove in a new job with a very diverse and international workforce. Here she was able to find her voice fairly soon. "I have had a very rapid rise. I made principal [in my early 30s]."

Anita's experience and others like hers suggest the importance of organizational commitment to creating more supportive work environments for diverse groups of people. Interestingly, Anita herself and several of the women we spoke to embrace Sandberg's language of self-help. In her capacity as a manager who evaluates a number of people in her office, Anita mentioned, "I don't want to hear complaining [from women] – do something about it and make things happen." However, when we consider her experience and the experiences of several other women we spoke to, we find that, in order to make things happen, you need not just individual initiative but also a shift in organizational attitudes. Deborah, Shobha and Anita herself all benefited from switching to more diverse work settings.

Interestingly, none of the women showed an interest in working in environments that had a high concentration of Indians. Rather, they sought jobs where the workforce had wide-ranging diversity. Interactions with a more diverse workforce, they felt, would create a better understanding of other cultural mores. There is keen interest in learning and adapting to a diversity of experiences and attitudes, rather than finding a space that provides for tight, co-ethnic bonding.

Family networks

Many of the women we interviewed also mentioned the importance of choosing a spouse who would be supportive of their professional mobility. As we noted earlier, for independent women migrants, family networks play a less immediate role in their immigrant journeys. Nonetheless, spousal support remains an important part of personal capital and one that can build into social capital (or lack thereof). Several, but not all, of the women that we interviewed arrived in the US single. Many of our respondents noted that being single was initially helpful in their careers, in that they could work long hours. However many also noted that having a partner enabled them to justify a "better work-life balance" and also develop additional social capital.

Towards that end, several women mentioned that they were conscious of choosing partners who understood and supported their professional interests. Having taken the first step of moving out of India independently, they chose to continue that route by independently seeking out supportive spouses. Ragini noted, for example, that her "parents pressured me to get married . . . but, by then, I held the cards in my hand, since I was half a world away. . . . I always wanted to marry an equal, I always knew that." Shobha's decision to overcome the visa-status fears and complain about the hostile manager at her second job was greatly influenced by support from her partner. "I was with my now-husband then, so I had more emotional stability to do that. I was ready to leave even though it would have affected my green card."

Having arrived in the US as a single woman, she eventually married an Indian man that she met through her family well after she had finished her master's program and begun her professional career in this country.

> My parents were OK with me being single for a few years, and then my mom got stressed about it. They didn't pressure, but they wanted to see me married. It was good to be isolated from the pressure of marriage in India.

Shobha notes that she got married "late in life" compared to other Indian women. She does not, however, see this as something to regret. Being able to stay away from that pressure in India allowed her to take her time and make a choice she was comfortable with.

Even our early immigrants benefited from having highly supportive spouses and partners. Uma met her eventual husband, also an Indian, at her university. He consistently encouraged her to carve out her own professional path. Uma recalls that even her husband's mother encouraged her to follow her professional ambitions. "My husband's mother was very supportive of my career," she recalled. "I think maybe she lived vicariously through my accomplishments."

At the same time, almost all the women we interviewed acknowledged that, for Indian women in their position, choosing a supportive spouse continued to be a challenging endeavor. Many remained sensitive to the fact that, in India, women often face a huge amount of family and social pressure to get married. Post-migration, the pressures are less but the choices are still limited. The lack of intersections in the interests of immigrant Indian men and women in the workplace that we described in the previous chapter seems to persist in the personal sphere as well.

Anita observed that for Indian women,

> I think the marriage expectations and cultural expectations are a big deal. If you are married, you need to have an understanding spouse. An Indian woman [in a very senior position] told me that she is single because she had not found someone who can understand her and support her career.

Finding a supportive spouse seems to be particularly challenging for those who arrive on work visas and are less familiar with cultural norms of dating. Mahi, a banker who moved to the US on an inter-company transfer in her thirties, continues to face ongoing pressure from her family to get married. Finding an Indian man who will be supportive of her work has been equally challenging in India and in the US. Mahi mentioned that since she did not experience university life in the US, she feels hesitant and unsure about the cultural context of dating in the US. Vani, who also migrated for work in her thirties, echoed a similar sentiment. "I wanted to get married, just didn't find anyone. It's not like women of my age in India were going out on dates."[9]

Even for those who do find supportive Indian spouses, the cultural norms and gender expectations that they sought to push against in India did not recede completely. Ragini said that she received "mixed support from husband. There is significant mobility related conflict as (my) husband travels a lot and his job compelled a move." While she moved to a different city for her husband's job, Ragini felt frustrated by a feeling that "I was being judged by his career." Kavita also noted that while her spouse was generally supportive, the issue of work-related travel has been a source of conflict.

> Eventually, my company will want me to relocate or to travel a lot. . . . This is something my husband will not agree to. . . . If I don't travel, my progress and career will be a conversation, not a done deal. It will stall.[10]

Conclusion

This chapter has shown us that the process of building professionally supportive networks has changed considerably across generations. Later generations of immigrants have benefited from the support of bigger and more sophisticated in-group networks. Arriving students, in particular, have access to institutionally supported groups that help acclimatize Indian and/ or a larger body of international students. Almost all the respondents who came to the US as students mentioned the support they received from other Indian students.[11] At the same time, as we have shown in this chapter, recent immigrants continue to be reminded of the networking barriers that arise because of national origin and gender as they transition from university life to work life.

Women across generations, from Uma in the 1960s to Shobha in the 2000s, are willing to find proactive pathways to overcome these barriers. They show determination, partially out of choice and partially out of necessity, to tackle the impediments they face. "My team did not know much about India, but they were curious," said one respondent.

> Some people had never even flown anywhere. . . . They were like my parents: It just takes time to get warmed up to you. . . . It can be annoying, and you have to learn, and they have to learn, too. Over time, we understood each other better.

Many of our women respondents are conscious of that the fact that their professional skills serve as their gateway to residence and success in the United States. As Asha said, "Your qualifications are the only reason for you to be here. It's your qualifications that make or break you. Your work is your capital." When faced with barriers and biases, our group of women have risen to the challenge and acquired as much capital as they could.

Yet, in these stories, we also see that individual voices, no matter how determined, tend to be drowned out unless they receive organizational and policy support. Early cohorts of women immigrants have benefited from government policies aimed at increasing opportunities for women, particularly in STEM fields. Later cohorts have realized that professional mobility is more feasible in organizations that have a more diverse workforce. Even as the women themselves seem to strongly identify with Sandberg's self-help language, they are not oblivious to the impact of their national origin and gender identities. On the contrary, many of them are acutely aware of the bias barriers that they face. This is represented in the multiple comments about the disadvantages of being seen as a "meek, Indian woman" or the difficulties of "talking sports."

Interestingly, despite the fact that they determinedly strove to move away from the gender constraints of life and work in India, a majority of the women we interviewed mentioned that they were not consciously feminist before they migrated. After encountering the post-migration racial and gendered challenges, particularly at work, many acknowledged that they began to think about their journey in feminist terms. Over time, they said, they began to be more consciously aware of the systemic changes that confront women in India and in the US. We explore this post-migration identity formation further in the next chapter. We also examine how and to what extent Indian immigrant women have been able to situate their individual and collective experiences within the larger social context of race and gender relations in the United States. As we will see, the pursuit of independence that prompted the initial migration choice continues well into the post-migration journeys of the women we chronicle.

Notes

1 Sandberg, Sheryl. 2013. *Lean in: Women, Work, and the Will to Lead.* New York: Knopf.
2 Interestingly, Sandberg herself discusses the valuable mentorship she received from Larry Summers. Summers, of course, is the former president of Harvard University who, as we noted in the previous chapter, is infamous for his statement about women in STEM fields.
3 Faludi, Susan. 2013. "Facebook Feminism, Like It or Not." *The Baffler 23.* http://www. thebaffler.com/salvos/facebook-feminism-like-it-or-not (accessed January 18, 2015).
4 Putnam, Robert. 1994. *Making Democracy Work: Civic Traditions in Modern Italy.* Princeton, NJ: Princeton University Press.
5 McGuire, Gail M. 2002. "Gender, Race, and the Shadow Structure: A Study of Informal Networks and Inequality in a Work Organization." *Gender and Society* 16 (3): 303–322; Mouw, Ted. 2003. "Social Capital and Finding a Job: Do Contacts Matter?" *American Sociological Review* 68 (6): 868–898.
6 Mitra, Diditi. 2012. "Social Capital Investment and Immigrant Economic Trajectories: A Case Study of Punjabi American Taxi Drivers in New York City." *International Migration* 50 (4): 67–84.
7 George, Sheba. 2005. *When Women Come First: Gender and Class in Transnational Migration.* Berkeley: University of California Press.
8 She also noted that such networks are not available to some other students of color, for example, first generation Latina students.
9 Vani mentioned that she eventually married a non-Indian man in the US introduced to her by a friend.
10 Eventually, Kavita did relocate with her family. Her husband agreed to leave his job to be with her and their children.
11 This was also the experience of Ramya and Bidisha, both of whom arrived in the US on student visas in the late 1990s.

5 Merging histories
Charting feminist journeys in the US and India

In 1896, Pandita Ramabai, a pioneering early Indian feminist and champion of women's education, embarked on a journey to the US that led to an early example of a universal, transnational feminist experience. Ramabai had been invited by Rachel Bodley, the dean of the Woman's Medical college of Pennsylvania, to witness the graduation ceremony of Anandibai Joshi. Dean Bodley, a product of the nascent American women's movement of the 19th century, was interested in building international linkages for women's education. While in the US, Ramabai published her essay *The High Caste Hindu Woman* as a fund-raising tool for a school for widows in India. The book described the gender constraints that limited the lives of Indian women in traditional upper-caste households.[1] With Bodley's help, Ramabai's cause came to be embraced widely by the early American feminists and generated much popular interest in the media as well.[2] But Ramabai was no mere passive protégé of the American feminists. A strong and independent social thinker in her own right, she returned the "American gaze"[3] by writing a critical anthropological account of American society. In her book, *The Peoples of The United States*, Ramabai presents an insightful discussion of social life in the US. While highlighting the positive egalitarian aspects of US society and the possibilities of an emerging woman's movement, Ramabai's keen gaze recognized and questioned the restrictive notions of femininity that constrained American women. She also recognized the central fissures in American society:

> The United States of America is famous for its wealth, education, and advancement, and with reason. But racial discrimination and prejudice, which are most inimical to all progress and civility, are not altogether absent in this country.[4]

Ramabai's early cross-national feminist journey reflects themes that remain relevant to the experiences of later generations of immigrant Indian women. In the previous chapters we saw that, across generations, Indian women immigrants are involved in the micropolitics of change at the individual level. Having pushed against the gendered limitations to life and work in India, they carry on this tradition when they encounter race and gender barriers in US workplaces. In this chapter, we will place the history of women and work at the center of our analysis and explore the intersection between these micro struggles and the broader feminist movement in both countries.

While our cohort of independent women immigrants have benefited from the advances made by the feminist movement in both India and the US, they are also active contributors to its progress in both countries. At the same time they also encounter the racial tensions that have tested the unity of the women's movement in the US. Interestingly, only a few of the women we interviewed acknowledged being consciously feminist before their immigrant journey, even though their migration choices were feminist in nature. Yet, we find that the gender and racial assumptions our respondents encountered in their post-immigrant lives have often led to a search for new identities as feminists and non-white immigrant women, opening up possibilities for a global feminist compact.

The reluctant feminists

"I did not consider myself a feminist on arrival. Feminism evolved over the years as coping with family, work, happiness." Ragini's response represents a pattern that emerged in our interviews. As we described in earlier chapters, many of our respondents were seeking more independence and opportunities than were available to women in India. Yet all but two of our respondents mentioned that they did not think of themselves as feminists. Nor did they identify with a collective struggle for expanding equality for women in any way prior to migration. Ayesha, the youngest woman in our cohort, echoes Ragini's sentiments. She came to the US to break free from the restrictive environment for girls in her family. "I was not even allowed to go down the street alone; girls were not to be heard in my family. I came to the US to experience a different life." Yet she mentioned, "I did not think of my decision as feminist." Rita adds, "I was not consciously a feminist in India – I don't think I was even aware of the word."

This reluctance to associate with feminism and the lack of awareness of the larger struggle for women's equality is not unique to middle-class Indian women. Ramya has often encountered the "I am not a feminist" refrain among her students, and it is also a much-discussed issue within the women's movement in the United States. In both countries, the distancing from the macro perspective of a collective struggle for women's opportunities is to some degree an outcome of the success of the movement itself. There is, in fact, a long and powerful history of a women's movement in India that runs parallel to and in many ways is comparable to the feminist movement in the United States.

The parallel histories of first-wave feminism

The early movement for women's empowerment in India can be traced to the mid-19th century. It emerged out of a larger social reform movement that was partly influenced by the exposure to western education introduced by British colonialism. The reform movement originated primarily among elite, Hindu upper-caste men with access to higher education.[5] They pushed for a reform of the ritualistic caste practices and divisions within Hindu society that they found to be incompatible with modern ideas about equality and human progress. Along the same lines they also came to see the severe restrictions on women's education and freedom as contrary to ideas of modern progress. They therefore became advocates for educating and empowering women in their own families. Anandibai Joshi and Gurubai Karmarkar's 19th-century journeys to the Women's Medical College of Pennsylvania were the outcome of this early advocacy for women's education. Similarly, Pandita Ramabai was also encouraged to pursue higher education by her father in the face of considerable opposition from the larger community.[6] Initially empowered by the men in their lives, these remarkable women subsequently made the cause their own and continued to advocate for education and expanded freedoms for women.[7]

As we have seen before, a few of these early feminists received support from the American women's movement. Often referred to as the first wave of feminism, the 19th-century women's movement in the US focused on expanding women's access to higher education and, more famously, on securing women's suffrage or the right to vote. In addition, many of the first-wave feminists like Elizabeth Cady Stanton and Francis Willard were also deeply engaged in larger social reform issues such as the anti-slavery movement. Taking an interest in women's progress and education globally was in keeping with these wider reformist interests. Thus emerged the connections between Indian visitors like Anandibai Joshi and Pandita Ramabai and the first-wave American feminists. Anandibai Joshi was mentored and supported in her journey by early feminists like Caroline Healey Dall, who eventually wrote a biography about Joshi's unique journey. Pandita Ramabia's mission of setting up schools for widows inspired the formation of "Ramabai circles" in various US cities, where they discussed her book and raised funds for her school. Pandita Ramabai herself gave public talks about her mission and efforts.[8]

This interest in the plight of Indian women can at times seem like a civilizing mission taken on by a benevolent West.[9] The Barbour Scholarship at the University of Michigan, an important conduit for Asian women seeking to pursue higher education in the US, illustrates this tendency. Established in 1914 at the bequest of a former alumnus Levi L. Barbour, the scholarship was specifically intended to provide Asian women with the opportunity to get a western education. Explaining his motivation for funding the scholarships, Levi L. Barbour wrote:

> The Idea of the Oriental girls' scholarships is to bring girls from the Orient, give them an Occidental education and let them take back whatever they found good and assimilate the blessings among the peoples from which they come.[10]

The statement makes clear the perspective of viewing the "Orient" as the exotic realm that required the civilizing influence of a western education. In this very colonial notion of educating the "Orient" there is no acknowledgment of the diverse perspectives the visiting women could offer to their hosts. However, when we look at the accounts of the interaction between the early Indian and American feminists written by the women themselves, we see a more nuanced interaction between individuals. In Caroline Healey Dall's biography of Anandibai Joshi and in other accounts of the interactions between Anandibai Joshi and Pandita Ramabai and the 19th-century American feminists, we see mutual respect and admiration for the pushing of the boundaries of possibilities for women in both countries. Moreover, both Joshi and Ramabai also retained a critical perspective on women's lives in the US even as they were inspired by the freedoms that were new to them. In addition to her critique of racial divisions, Ramabai wrote critically about the preoccupation with fashion and materialism among American women.[11] At the same time, she also wrote of her interactions with stalwarts of this first-wave feminism like the well-known suffragist leader Francis Willard. Her accounts of these interactions are one of a remarkably equal engagement and exchange. In this early interaction, therefore, we see a true transnational exchange of ideas and hopes for a global women's movement.[12]

In the 20th century, the nascent women's movement in India was subsumed within the nationalist movement against British colonialism. As the Indian nationalist movement began to gain strength, the social reform movement at times had to make a choice between opposing the colonial government and supporting some of the progressive reform laws it supported. For example, Pandita Ramabai's status as an admired and pioneering advocate for women's empowerment began to fade during this time because she had converted to Christianity and had accepted missionary support for higher education. Viewing this as a rejection of Indian values, support for Ramabai's advocacy diminished as the Indian nationalist movement gained momentum.

Bidisha recalls the experience of women in her family as being indicative of this delicate balance. Bidisha's family belongs to the *shudra* caste, the lowest caste category in the Hindu hierarchy. The reform movement of the 19th century provided a way for her family to break free of some of the oppressive conditions prescribed for their caste. By the early 20th century, this resulted in her maternal great-grandmother becoming the first in her generation to be literate. Her great-grandfather was educated as a lawyer and took an active role in the Hindu reform movement, as it pertained to his caste group. Her grandmother's ability to use her education, on the other hand, was more circumscribed. She recounted to Bidisha that women were expected to use their education only to read Hindu religious texts and were explicitly forbidden from reading reform literature that addressed women's emancipation.

The ability to read religious texts represented a big departure from the past generations, where this would have been forbidden to her caste members. The Hindu reform movement was pivotal in campaigning for wider access across castes to Hindu texts. However, nationalists and reformers remained divided on supporting British progressive laws on women's education and empowerment. Bidisha's great-grandmother engaged in her own micropolitics to subvert her family's strictures. She hid novels that addressed women's rights and social reform within the covers of religious texts. In this way, she was able to read books that were prohibited to her. "Your great-grandfather wanted me to only read about religion," she reminisced. "But I wanted to see what was out there. What was all the chatter about changing things? Are things going to change for women, too? I wanted to know."

After India gained independence in 1947, the terrain shifted once again. The Constitution of India made no distinction between men and women in terms of basic citizenship rights. The guarantee of the right to vote and the explicit recognition of men and women as equal citizens in the Indian constitution have been referred to as a remarkable step forward for women's rights. In contrast, women acquired such political rights in the US only after a protracted struggle waged by the women's suffrage movement.[13] The constitutional and legal framework that emerged soon after independence was supportive of equal rights for women in other realms as well. The science and technology resolution that linked the promotion of science education to the goals of economic development used language that made clear that both men and women would contribute to science and development. For example, the resolution explicitly specified that it sought to "[e]nsure that the creative talent of men and women is encouraged and finds full scope in scientific activity."[14] This stands in strong contrast to the sustained period of collective political action that was required to secure such equal treatment for women in higher education in the US.

It was this era of progressive political reforms that allowed women like E. K. Janaki Ammal and Sarkeshwari Agha, who returned to India with advanced degrees from the US, to move into crucial leadership roles in education and science research institutes in India. E. K. Janaki Ammal obtained her master's in botany from the University of Michigan in 1925, aided by the Barbour Scholarship. She returned to India from Michigan and had a trailblazing career as a botanist, helping to set up major national research institutes in her field in post-independence India. Soon after Janaki Ammal, in the 1928–29 academic year, Sharkeshwari Agha from Allahabad was granted the Barbour Scholarship. After her time as the Barbour fellow, Sarkeshwari Agha returned to India in 1930 and headed various national-level commissions on women's education and was also involved in the administration of the Allahabad University.[15]

Their success, and that of other women like them, made women in positions of power a presence in India. As we have seen in Chapter 1, this legacy has continued, with more women in positions of power in the political and corporate sphere in India in comparison to the US.

A consequence of this post-independence shift in the legal and constitutional protections for women was that grassroots activism around women's rights became more muted. There was less identification with a feminist struggle, particularly among educated middle-class women who were absorbed into the expanding opportunities in the public sector. Women's organizations during this early post-independence period were more likely to be aligned and sponsored by the government rather than activist in nature.[16] It is perhaps this history that is reflected in the reluctance of our group of middle-class women to identify explicitly with a feminist cause. At the same time, it is also this early history of women's rights in India that helps us understand how the trend of independent women migrants emerges as early as the 1960s. Women like Usha who were pioneers even in the American higher education system in the 1960s follow from this history of early support for women's empowerment in India. Even when the activist spirit was muted in the aftermath of independence, there was an undercurrent of awareness about progress on women's rights among the middle class. Rekha, who came to the US in 1975, exemplifies this tradition. She mentioned that she did not consider herself a feminist before migration. "I was not really politically attuned. My feminist and race consciousness was found here." But when asked if her awareness of feminist issues only began post-migration, she countered, "That would be harsh; I would say that the language of feminists was not entirely alien to me, but it was not entirely conscious either. I came from a family of active, educated women, so there was some awareness."

The language versus the spirit of feminism

A second wave of activist feminism did emerge in India in the 1970s. This was prompted by the realization that while the legal and political framework seemed liberal, the actual implementation of these legal protections was very sparse. Most of the benefits seemed confined to elite or middle-class women who could take advantage of new laws. On the other hand, there seemed to be limited efforts at opening up education and access to the large majority of poor and marginalized women. A 1974 report of the Committee on the Status of Women provided particularly stark evidence on the worsening conditions of well-being for women, particularly among the poor. Gender disparities in education and employment had in fact continued to widen in the post-independence era. Even among middle-class women there was a realization that, while the legal framework was supportive of political rights in the public sphere, very little had changed in the private or domestic sphere. Issues of domestic violence, particularly around the practice of dowry, had received little active support from law enforcement. Similarly, inheritance laws, which apply differently to different religious groups, continued to favor men.

As a reaction, sparks of activism emerged in different parts of the country to protest particularly egregious cases of disenfranchisement and violence. Such activism was intense and usually tied to specific issues and injustices, particularly among poor and marginalized women.[17] Many of these movements have had a pioneering impact on the possibilities of feminist organization globally. For example, the Self Employed Women's Association (SEWA), formed in 1973, was a visionary women's trade union. SEWA's mission was to organize poor women who worked predominantly in informal forms of employment for daily wages without the security of formal contracts, salaries and benefits. SEWA's work provided the inspiration and the model for organizing informal sector workers in many developing economies. Similarly, the Chipko movement has achieved near legendary status as the precursor to the modern eco-feminism movement. Chipko was a form of protest adopted by rural women to protest rapid deforestation in the foothills of the Himalayas. This was having a devastating impact on the lives of the women who depended on the forests for food and fuel sources. In 1973, a group of women attached themselves to the trees to prevent them from being cut. The word Chipko literally meant to attach, and it is from this term and movement that we derive the phrase "tree-huggers."

While influential and pioneering at a global level, these movements did not create a cohesive national feminist movement. Within India, they were viewed as localized protests to express concerns about the failure of post-independence development strategies to deliver benefits beyond the traditional elites. As such they did not foster a cohesive sense of feminist identity across different caste and class groups. By the 1990s, women's causes became even more splintered across religious and caste lines. In India, personal laws that govern marriage, divorce and inheritance are different for different religions groups. These variations became a flash point in the late '80s and '90s and set up conflicts that called for a choice between religious allegiance and advances in women's rights. The rise of a religious right also gave rise to what some authors describe as right-wing feminism. Such movements sought to present a contrast between western feminism and women's roles derived from what they viewed as more traditional Indian values.[18] An additional wedge was created when attempts to expand caste-based affirmative action quotas for government jobs and public universities sparked massive protests in the 1990s and polarized debates about many social issues, including gender, along caste line.

These contrasting agendas limited the development of a unified language of feminism or even a general feminist identification. We see this reflected in the lack of feminist identification among the later generations of middle-class women migrants we interviewed. Some of our respondents spoke more directly about the problems of caste and class identifications that they encountered. Reena's family belongs to a Scheduled Tribe (ST). Scheduled Tribes are a constitutionally recognized group of tribal and indigenous communities, also known as *adivasis*, in India. STs are among the most socially, politically and economically deprived groups in India. As such, they are provided certain protections under Indian law, including preferential access to educational institutions and jobs and protection from discrimination.[19] Reena spoke about the burden of caste identification that at times set her apart from her peers,

> My family is ST. . . . There were embarrassing moments. Like, in my . . . school, some teachers would call on us and say all the SC/ST students stand up and pay your lower tuition now. Then the whole class would know. I have enjoyed the freedom from that here, the lack of boundaries, those unseen, unsaid boundaries of caste and tribe in India.

Despite the polarizing influence of caste, religion and class, however, the intensity of activism by women's groups, even if localized in nature, ensured that the discussion about women's empowerment could not be entirely ignored and continued to remain pertinent in India. Padma reflected on this inherent sense of awareness among Indian women, "Being in the US, we learn that we were feminists early on but did not know the words, the language." Padma completed her PhD and eventually became an established scholar. Reflecting on women academics, she noted,

> As it were, in South Asian studies, there are a number of strong academic feminists. South Asian scholars seem to have a disproportionately high representation in women's studies. I don't know why. Maybe because we are aware of gender studies on coming here or quickly become aware of it.

Encounters with feminist narratives after migration

A cohesive feminist language and identity did not evolve smoothly in the US, either. The first-wave feminists focused on expanding legal political rights for women. They finally achieved a major victory in 1920 when the 19th amendment to the US constitution secured full voting rights for women. However, in the next few decades opportunities for women to participate in the broader political and economic life was slow despite the establishment of legal rights. By the 1960s, a simmering discontent exploded into the second wave of feminism. The movement was given its initial voice with the 1963 publication of Betty Friedan's seminal book, the *Feminine Mystique*.[20] In the book, Friedan highlighted the intense pressure women faced to focus singularly on raising the perfect nuclear family and suppress all other ambitions and talents. She spoke of the dissatisfaction and depression that many educated women with limited opportunities for their talents experienced.

Friedan's work spurred a wave of activism that sought to expand employment and other opportunities for women to participate equally in civic and economic life. The year 1963 also saw the passing of the historic Equal Pay Act, which prohibited gender discrimination in pay. However, the second-wave feminists wanted more than mere laws that were often not enforced vigilantly. They believed in continuing activism to put pressure on the government and employers to make active changes. Friedan herself participated in the creation of the National Organization for Women (NOW) in 1966. NOW became the catalyst in pushing for change. It is this activism that resulted in the kind of active government pressure for expanding opportunities for women scientists that Uma and Jaya described and benefited from. By asking to be taken more seriously at work, Uma in her own way carried forward the work of the second-wave feminists and paved the way for the next generation of women scientists.

However, later generations of immigrant women in our cohort had limited awareness of the pioneering achievements of the second-wave feminism that made their own career trajectories possible. This awareness gap is perhaps to be expected given that, by the 1980s, the fervor of second-wave feminism in the US seemed to fade, due to a variety of reasons. The increasing popularity of a conservative political ideology brought with it a right-wing women's activism that sought to valorize women's traditional roles as homemakers. A contentious fight over an Equal Rights Amendment to the constitution in the late 1970s and early 1980s was emblematic of this conservative activism. The equal rights amendment, an idea first debated in the 1920s, aimed to enshrine gender equality in all laws in the constitution. Dissatisfied at the pace of reform and the weak implementation of the Equal Pay Act, NOW launched a concerted effort through the 1970s to revive the cause of an equal rights amendment as a way to expand opportunities for women in all spheres of economic and political life.

While initially successful, the issue began to lose support due to a counter-campaign led by conservative women's activist Phyllis Schlafly. Schlafly portrayed the Equal Rights Amendment as discrediting and devaluing the importance of the traditional roles of women as wives and mothers. Her movement succeeded to a certain extent in portraying NOW and the second-wave feminists as out of touch, unfeminine radicals who denied all natural differences between men and women. In her book *Backlash*, feminist author Susan Faludi describes how this conservative attempt at equating feminists with a militant rejection of femininity diminished the movement's focus on expanding rights and opportunities for women.[21] It also created a backlash against acknowledging a feminist identity and brought with it the pressure to cultivate a more feminine appearance and affect.

This emphasis on a particular kind of femininity was noted as a puzzle by some of our respondents. Sonali came to the US to pursue a doctoral degree after having had a successful career in India. She noted,

> I have noticed that women in social circles here don't really think of their intellectual prowess as part of their identity as a complete woman. It wasn't like that for me in the [professional world] in India. Here, I would go to a bar with other faculty, and I would see the woman, someone I looked up to, dumb herself down for flirting. People would tell me to not tell men that I am [highly educated]. A lot of women here don't see their professional success as a part of their appeal as a woman.

Similarly, Vani, a software engineer, noted that while there was gender bias in both India and the US, in the US there was more emphasis on the appearance of the women. "But being a short, dumpy woman does not help here; being tall and blonde does help. Appearances matter."

Moving from middle-class privilege to minority status

Beyond the conservative challenge, second-wave feminism also had to contend with yet another major fault line. The galvanizing issue for second-wave feminists was the limited opportunities for women to utilize their education and talents outside the home. Friedan specifically spoke about the emptiness and the lack of worth experienced by educated women confined to the home. Implicit in this narrative was the assumption that the women came from households that could afford to have them stay at home. The women Friedan and NOW were advocating for, therefore, were essentially middle-class and upper-middle-class women who were predominantly white. As noted feminist scholar bell hooks pointed out, "When Friedan wrote *The Feminine Mystique*, more than one-third of all women were in the work force."[22] A majority of African American women had no choice but to work for a living.[23] By focusing entirely on expanding work opportunities, therefore, Friedan's brand of feminism focused singularly on the concerns of upperclass white women. Hooks notes that "[m]asses of women were concerned about economic survival, ethnic and racial discrimination, etc." Such concerns did not find prominence in the agenda of the second-wave feminists.

Rekha, whose immigrant journey began in1975, echoed this feeling of not finding a place on the mainstream feminist agenda, "I went to a meeting [of feminists in the US] and my friend and I were the only brown women there. I felt my issues and their issues were not the same." In Chapter 4, we also saw that even among the more recent cohorts of immigrant woman, the subtle discrimination of assumptions that they encounter at work was not only about gender but also about race. In fact, quite a few of our respondents articulated that their encounters with the interconnected racial and gendered assumptions led them to develop a consciousness about needing a space and voice of their own. Rekha described her moment of awakening when, as a teaching assistant, she would encounter students who were skeptical about her abilities.

> The students would look at me as if you to say, "Who are you to teach me English?" It was there that I learned about teaching. It was there that I saw the intersection of race and gender and there that I found my racial and feminist awakening.

Rekha went on to become active in advocating for the rights of South Asian women in the US.

Like Rekha, encountering questions about their abilities due to gendered and racial assumptions seems to be a turning point in awakening a conscious activism among quite a few of our respondents. Shobha's experiences with unsupportive managers led her to become an active participant in Asian networking groups. These groups, Shobha mentioned, helped her become more self-aware and cognizant of issues specific to Asian women in workplaces. Reena's difficult encounters around race at the workplace led her to form a South Asian media forum to present works related to South Asian experiences. Mira recalled facing issues similar to Rekha in the classroom: "There were issues with being a woman of color, for example, students not liking my accent." Interestingly, while Indian immigrant women in academia encounter student skepticism about accents and abilities in the US, foreign, particularly western faculty visiting India experience the opposite. Both Bidisha and Ramya recall discussions with their US colleagues who find the curiosity and welcome shown by students in India on their exchange programs to be refreshing.[24]

Mira eventually formed an association of Indian scholars within her field. Reflecting on her involvement with the association, Mira made an interesting observation: "I never thought I would hang out with *desis* (Indians), but it's a neat group and we even meet every two years in India. It always helps to know people." The middle-class privilege that our cohort of women had access to in India largely insulated them from the need to be active in support groups and other organized movements. As Mira articulated, few think of needing such support. But the post-migration reality that Indian women seem to encounter is that, as women of color, they are the outsiders now and have to work harder to prove their abilities. This therefore prompts an active search for social networks and alliances.

Race, class and gender

The possibilities for new alliances within the existing networks of women's groups are limited for Indian women, given their unique circumstances. While there is a sense of dissonance with white women, there is also little commonality of experience with other women of color. Though the migration experience results in a loss of class privilege, their middle-class backgrounds nonetheless sets them apart from African American women and many other immigrant women of color. Jaya, one of the earliest immigrants in our group, described the awareness of class privilege that she developed in 1970s. At her first job in Atlanta, Jaya decided to take on the evening shift since it offered more pay. She found that while the day shift staff "were mostly white or Indian, the night shift were black women." The night shift offered more pay and also free dinner. It was then that Jaya realized, "The experience of African Americans is different from Indians." In more recent years, the experiences of middle-class Indian immigrants have also diverged from more impoverished immigrant groups from Central and South America. A few in our group were well aware of this difference. Padma cautioned,

> We must recognize that our trajectories, as Indian women, are different. We tend to come from middle-class families with a heavy emphasis on education. I see that a first generation Latina women doctoral student is going to have significantly more challenges than a first generation Indian woman – language, education, everything.

In his book *The Karma of Brown Folk*, Vijay Prashad has argued that India immigrants as a group have tended not to recognize this difference in class privilege. Instead, the post-1965 generation of Indian immigrants has embraced the myth of a "model minority" that has often been used to portray African Americans in a negative light in comparison. Missing in the model minority narrative is the reality that due to the skill-based immigration quotas, Indian immigrants belong to the "cream of the bourgeois South Asian crop,"[25] who bring with them the class and education privileges that have been systematically denied to African Americans and other marginalized minority groups.

At the same time, independent Indian immigrant women do not necessarily find a natural space within the model minority picture. That picture encompasses more traditional gender roles, where the men are the professionals and the women are associational migrants whose primary responsibilities are within the household. There is therefore a limited platform for seeking support for the kinds of interconnected racial and gender issues that Indian professional women are facing. Their concentration in STEM-related industries is particularly isolating as well. Vani, who migrated in 1998, explained, "The first black woman I have every worked with in my whole career in the US was in 2013. I have worked with Asian women, but on the whole there are very few women in my industry." Anu concurred, "There are not many women or women of color in my position. There aren't very many Hispanics in consulting overall. I do work with Indian and Asian women, but not many at the principal level."

Mira related yet another teaching incident that illuminates the uncomfortable position of India women in the class, gender and race hierarchy in the US. While her white students had issues with her accent and ability as a woman of color, students of color had other issues. While working on her PhD, Mira worked at a tutoring program for African American and Latino inner city kids. "You could see that life had beaten them so much that they wanted to beat you back. They . . . didn't accept me as a minority. It was an exercise in humility for me."

Finding the common ground: third-wave feminism?

In a 1992 essay in the feminist magazine *Ms*, Rebecca Walker introduced the term "third-wave feminism."[26] Walker and other third-wave feminists attempt to move beyond the divisive rhetoric of the previous movements. Some third-wave feminists believe that there are natural differences between men and women and make an effort to reclaim femininity. Other third-wave feminists recognize that women, feminists and people of color have experienced, at different times, multiple positions and identities. In an effort to reconcile these different and, at times, conflicting identities, third-wave feminists have tended to move away from specific political agendas that reflect the claims and demands of any one group of women. Instead, they favored individual personal narratives that focus on the micropolitics or the day-to-day lived experience of gender.

The impact and direction of the third-wave feminists continues to be an ongoing debate. Within the framework of plural identities and the everyday experiences of gender, we do find a commonality of interests and concerns that independent Indian women migrants can relate to. This is particularly the case given the changes in priorities and concerns that we see emerging among our cohort of women in their post-migrant lives. The micropolitics that immigrant woman engage in prior to migration are mostly concerned with pushing the boundaries of gendered opportunities outside the home. Independent migration represents a significant victory in that endeavor. Post-migration, a new micropolitics seems to have emerged for our group of women pertaining to issues within the home and maintaining a balance between the home and work. This micropolitics is common ground for most professional women in the US.

For our group of women, the emergence of these concerns of a home life seems to come as a surprise, given their intrepid pre-migration experience of rejecting gendered boundaries. A majority of our responders also arrived single and had not given much thought to the conflicting priorities of home and work. When confronted with this new question, some of our respondents were circumspect in their analysis of the changes they have begun to accept to create work life balance. Deborah believes that "Women's priorities change when they choose to have a family. Some people call that a sacrifice. I don't think it's a sacrifice; it's a choice we make and then we figure out how to balance family and work."

Others were more forthright in questioning why it always falls on women to make the changes in priorities. Ragini explained that she began to be concerned with these issues after getting married, when the question of whose career would be perceived as more important began to emerge.

> In many decisions, I felt short-changed and asked myself, "How did I reach this point?" I really started evaluating this question after having a daughter and considered the issues in raising boys vs. raising girls. I created a support group of mothers. I also started my blog as a rebellion against gender issues that I faced and want to assert my independence in income and position.

In considering these questions, Ragini realized that though she never considered herself a feminist when she arrived in the US, "My feminism evolved over the years as coping with family, work, happiness."

Shanta arrived in the US to pursue an undergraduate education. She was one of the few among our respondents to acknowledge a feminist identity prior to migration. "I definitely pursued a feminist orientation, minored in women's studies. I did, in part, come to the US to declare independence from my parents." Shanta eventually pursued an MBA degree from a highly ranked institution and married out of her choice. Yet she acknowledges that she now confronts new issues about her career,

> Marriage has not impacted my professional experience, but having a child has. I have been seeking entrepreneurial opportunities, but start-ups are not open to family issues. They are single, young, work crazy hours and don't really want to hear that you have a family.

With these varied reactions, our cohort of women is joining the conversations about an important unresolved concern stemming from the second-wave feminism. While the effort to expand opportunities for women outside the house was the primary focus of second-wave feminism, there was little opportunity to address the issue of what would happen within the household once such opportunities were available. As more middle-class women began to enter the workforce, this issue became a source of considerable friction between the ambitions of women of privilege, who were mostly white, and women of color, whose labor began to be used at home to support such ambitions.[27] Ultimately, as more recent generation of feminists have emphasized, this dilemma can only be addressed by expanding the scope of the question beyond being merely a woman's issue. The involvement and responsibility – or lack thereof – of men in this conversation is the crucial missing element in an issue that should be of broader concern, transcending lines of class and race. By actively reflecting on the gender relations within households and workplace, women like Ragini and Shanta are important new voices in this conversation.

Conclusion

In this chapter, as we traced the links between the micropolitics of immigrant women and the larger macropolitics of the organized women's movement, we once again see the power of expanding narratives. We find that varied individual battles and efforts, even if they are supported by class privilege, can contribute to the collective history of expanding opportunities. At the same time, individual battles and victories of expanding choices are often situated within and supported by collective and historical efforts.

Beginning with Ramabai's ground-breaking effort in the 19th century, we also see the possibilities of a common global feminist compact. Transcending the unequal dynamic of colonial interactions between the west and the orient, Ramabai was able to carve out a remarkable equality of purpose for a global women's cause. Recent decades have seen many more seemingly unbridgeable differences along class and race lines. Yet a common ground does emerge when we consider that many among our group of women are path breakers in their field even in more recent years. The quest for access to wider professional spaces for women is far from complete, and each pioneering story represents a widening of the space globally.

Notes

1 The subject of patriarchy and caste has been explored in more recent feminist studies. See, for example, Chakravarti, Uma. 2003. *Gendering Caste: Through a Feminist Lens.* Kolkata: Stree Publications; Fruzetti, Lina M. 1993. *The Gift of a Virgin: Women, Marriage, and Ritual in a Bengali Society.* New Delhi: Oxford University Press.
2 *New York Times.* 1888. "The Pandita Speaking on Behalf of Her Sisters." February 17.
3 Kosambi, Meera. 2002. "Returning the American Gaze: Pandita Ramabai's the Peoples of the United States, 1889." *Meridians* 2 (2): 188–212.
4 Kosambi 2002, p. 204.
5 Guha Ghosal, Sarbani. 2005. "Major Trends of Feminism in India." *The Indian Journal of Political Science* LXVI (4): 793–812.
6 Kosambi 2002.
7 Forbes, Geraldine. 1994. "Medical Careers and Health Care for Indian Women: Patterns of Control." *Women's History Review* 3 (4): 515–530; Chakravarti, Uma. 1998. *Rewriting History: The Life and Times of Pandita Ramabai.* New Delhi: Kali for Women.
8 *New York Times* 1888.

9 Gurjarpadhye, Prachi. 2014. "Through a Changing Feminist Lens: Three Biographies of Anandibai Joshi." *Economic & Political Weekly* 49 (33): 37–40.
10 Rufus, Carl W. 1942. "Twenty-Five Years of the Barbour Scholarships." *Michigan Alumnus Quarterly Review* 49 (11): 15.
11 Celarent, Barbara. 2011. "The High Caste Hindu Woman. Rev. of *Pandita Ramabai's America: Conditions of Life in the United States (United Stateschi Lokasthiti ani Pravasvritta)*." *American Journal of Sociology* 117 (1): 353–360.
12 Kosambi 2002.
13 Chitnis, Suma. 2004. "Feminism: Indian Ethos and Indian Convictions." In *Feminism in India*, ed. Maitrayee Chaudhuri. New Delhi: Kali for Women: 8–25.
14 Government of India. 1958. *Scientific Policy Resolution 1958.* http://dst.gov.in/stsysindia/spr1958.htm (accessed December 30, 2015).
15 Rufus 1942.
16 Sen, Samita. 2000. "Toward a Feminist Politics? The Indian Women's Movement in Historical Perspective." *The World Bank Policy Research Report on Gender and Development Working Paper Series No. 9.*
17 Sen 2000.
18 Sen 2000; Guha Ghoshal 2005.
19 Members of Scheduled Tribes (ST) and Scheduled Castes (SC) receive legal, preferential treatment in order address their historical disadvantages in Indian society. Members of SCs must be Hindu, Muslim, Sikh or Buddhist by religion; STs can belong to any religion.
20 Friedan, Betty. 1963. *The Feminine Mystique*. New York: W.W. Norton.
21 Faludi, Susan. 1991. *Backlash: The Undeclared War Against American Women.* New York: Crown.
22 hooks, bell. 2000. *Feminist Theory: From Margin to Center*. Boston: South End Press, p. 2.
23 Halley, Jean, Amy Eshleman, and Ramya Mahadevan Vijaya. 2011. *Seeing White: An Introduction to White Privilege and Race*. Lanham, MD: Rowman & Littlefield.
24 An interesting discussion of the social, economic, and racial dimensions of how migrants are perceived is provided in Koutin, Mawuva Remarque. 2015. "Why Are White People Expats While the Rest of Us Are Immigrants?" http://www.theguardian.com/global-development-professionals-network/2015/mar/13/white-people-expats-immigrants-migration (accessed December 30, 2015).
25 Prashad 2001, p. 169.
26 Walker, Rebecca. 1992. "Becoming the Third Wave." *Ms.*
27 hooks 2000.

6 Learning from the past and shaping new legacies

Kalpana Chawla was born in 1962 in the north Indian city of Karnal. After obtaining an engineering degree from Punjab Engineering College in 1982, she moved to the United States to pursue graduate studies. She attended the University of Texas at Arlington and obtained a doctoral degree from the University of Colorado. Chawla joined the National Aeronautics and Space Administration (NASA) in 1994.[1] Her contributions to space research at NASA have made her a household name in India, where countless children are regularly exhorted to "study hard, so that you can be like Kalpana Chawla one day." On February 3, 2003, at the age of 41, Kalpana Chawla died, along with six other astronauts, on the Space Shuttle Columbia. Chawla's journey ended tragically early, but her life continues to be an inspiration to millions of Indian school children, particularly girls. According to news reports, Chawla encountered and overcame family resistance to her decision to move to the US as single woman. Similar to the mothers of those whom we have profiled, Chawla's mother encouraged her to pursue her professional aspirations.[2] Chawla's accomplishments are a powerful illustration of how far Indian women have come on their independent immigrant journeys. In our concluding chapter, we will revisit some of our stories in order to understand the individual and societal factors that have made such remarkable journeys possible.

Kalpana Chawla is arguably the most well-known independent Indian woman immigrant to the United States.[3] There are others, as well, who serve as successful role models for women and immigrants alike. Indra K. Nooyi, born in the southern city of Chennai, became president and CEO of Pepsi Co in 2006. She was educated at the prestigious Indian Institute of Management, Kolkata. After working for a few years in India, Nooyi left to pursue graduate studies at Yale. Padmasree Warrior joined Cisco in 2008 as the company's chief technology and strategy officer, one of the senior-most women in the technology industry.[4] She was born and raised in the southern Indian city of Vijayawada. Warrior received her education at the Indian Institute of Technology and Cornell University.

Chawla, Nooyi and Warrior challenge many of the traditional notions of the Indian woman, whether it is Apu's wife in *The Simpsons*, the lonely housewives of Lahiri's novels and short stories or the prevailing depiction of women of color in positions of domestic servitude. One could dismiss the stories of women like Chawla, Nooyi and Warrior as simple extensions of the Indian "model immigrant story." But, of course, by virtue of their gender, they are not mere extensions of a larger narrative of success. In both India and the US, women in the role of space scientists, CEOs and CTOs are still an anomaly. The presence of women of color in such positions is even more rare. One could also suggest that these particular women are unique, products of significant, even exceptional, talent, ambition and luck. One of our respondents stated that "Indra Nooyi is an exception, she is not like the rest of us." However, in our study, we show that Nooyi's journey, while certainly notable, is not unique. The narratives that we have chronicled in this book show us that, in fact, there are numerous women, representing a diversity of age, profession and background, who have made similar journeys as professional, independent women.

In recognizing these multiple threads of professional drive and achievement, we also see the patterns of the larger fabric. Chawla, Nooyi and Warrior were all outstanding students in India who came to the US to pursue graduate education. The same commitment to exceling in studies can be found in the stories of Uma, Padma and Ragini. The family and societal expectations that led to skepticism of Chawla and Nooyi's initial decisions resonate in the stories of Reena and Ayesha. In our respondents, we see women who recount similar stories of cross-cultural miscommunication and eventual understanding; of the discrimination of assumptions and the successful challenges to those assumptions; of finding life partners who support the expansion, rather than narrowing, of choices; of consciously encouraging others – and, above all, of ambition, spirit and resilience.

Choosing to leave

All of the women in our primary set of respondents made a conscious decision to seek out an independent migratory pathway to the United States. Uma and Jaya started their journeys around the time of the enactment of the 1965 Immigration and Naturalization Act. In their recounting, we are reminded of how unusual it was for women of their generation to travel to the United States alone. Because her sister already lived in the US, Jyoti's decision was more readily accepted by her family. Here, we also see the application of micropolitics within Jyoti's family. Uma was unusual in her family in her interest in the sciences but was fortunate to have the support of older women in the family. Once again, an intergenerational support system enabled Uma to take steps that were unprecedented in her community.

In later decades, we see an expansion of choices for the women, but we also see continuing boundaries and restrictions. Rekha, who first arrived in the US in 1975, said that the US "was in our heads"; there was an expectation that you had to go. This was not, however, necessarily the norm. Kalpana Chawla came to the US in 1982, seven years after Rekha. Yet her choice was considered unusual for a woman of her background.[5] By the time Sujatha came to the United States in 2001, coming to the US was what you "had to do." She believed that, had she not come to the US for employment, she would have been marked as a "loser" among her peers in India. Yet Kavita, who also came in 2001, reports considerable opposition from her father. In the different narratives of the women, we can see the variable micropolitics of making the choice to leave.

Rising above or hitting the glass ceiling?

As they strived to build their careers in the United States, the women we interviewed continued to face what Uma called the discrimination of assumptions. Uma herself faced many instances of such discrimination. As a student, she found herself at a university that had only recently opened its doors to women. As a respected scientist, she advocated for more women being invited to travel on scientific expeditions. The determination that Uma showed in challenging prevailing assumptions is a powerful illustration of the incremental ways in which the micropolitics of the workplace can lead to substantive change.

Like Uma, Padmasree Warrior came to the United States in pursuit of higher studies in STEM. As the chief technology and strategy officer at Cisco Systems, Warrior became one of the most successful women in corporate America. Her achievements are particularly notable in the context of concerns about the low representation of women in technology. Uma and Padmasree's arrivals in the United States were separated by about two decades. One could argue that their successes in fields traditionally dominated by men shows us that the glass ceiling can, and has, been broken. That would be a hasty conclusion. Compared to Uma, Warrior would have found, in the US, an economy and society more receptive to women in the sciences. Still, today, only about 23 percent of Cisco's employees are female. In fact, the consistently low rates of female representation in the American technology sector has been subject to widespread media coverage.[6] When Warrior first joined the American workforce with a job at the venerable Motorola, she herself noted that she was one of only a handful of women at the company when she joined, which made it a "really daunting experience."[7] Recall that Warrior had stellar academic credentials from two reputed institutions – the Indian Institute of Technology and Cornell. Yet she had early doubts about her ability to succeed in the industry: "I . . . was not sure whether I could be successful in a work environment that, back then, and today still, was very male dominated," she said.[8] Today, conscious of her status as one of the relatively few (albeit growing) number of women who have attained the pinnacle of success in her field, Warrior is a "passionate supporter of all women in business and a staunch advocate of the global STEM initiative."[9] Like Uma, Warrior made her own mark in the American workforce and is now continuing the effort to diversify the American workplace. Almost all of the women in STEM, it should be noted, benefited enormously from state-funded higher education in India.

What, then, of women in non-STEM professions? We noted earlier that, in India, state policy and societal expectations have merged to create a very strong preference for STEM education. In the United States, as well, immigration policies have tended to lean in favor of students and workers with STEM skills. This means that there are relatively few women entering the United States in non-technology fields. The ones that do often find complicated journeys. Rekha, for example, was an accomplished journalist in India but could not find a comparable job here. Asha had strong academic credentials from the UK but faced visa-related barriers to finding reliable employment in higher education in the US. Rekha and Padma both discussed the racial stereotyping that can occur in academic institutions. At the same time, they noted that women from India who are entering the fields of the humanities and the social sciences face distinct advantages, as compared to other women of color. They tend to be familiar with English because of the emphasis on that language in the Indian education system. As a corollary to that, comfort with English also tends to imply that the person came from a comfortable middle-class, upper-middle-class or wealthy family in India.[10] Rekha recalls that she had a "sense of entitlement and privilege" and was taken aback by some of the racial and cultural stereotyping that she faced. Kavita remembers her first job in the United States was working with a union and notes that it was an "interesting" experience because "they had never really worked with an Indian woman, and they seemed quite surprised by my accent." In a very different work environment, Vani, who works in an engineering firm, notes that her colleagues and clients are often surprised by her fluency in English. These shifts in advantage and disadvantage, feelings of entitlement and experiences of discrimination create fascinating, multilayered experiences of immigration and assimilation.

Creating their own zone of comfort

Some women find humorous ways in which to address the micropolitics of identity. Rekha, for example, remembers, "I used to wear saris a lot while teaching. Sometimes students and others would look at me [and wonder], 'Can she really speak English?' After a while, I began to enjoy it, it was my form of resistance." Interestingly, this experience echoes that of Indra Nooyi's much-discussed experiences of wearing saris in the American corporate world. Nooyi has famously noted that, when she started her first summer job in the US, she wore saris because she could not afford to buy business suits. She notes, however, that

> I have never worn a saree to board meetings. . . . I think I have never shied away from the fact that I am an Indian and I don't intend to, but you can be at home with both cultures.[11]

In different ways, both Nooyi and Rekha have challenged their audiences to rethink assumptions about attire, language and other markers of national origin and race. These are examples of the micropolitics of change that occur at the intersection of the personal and the professional.

An interesting finding presented in this book is that, across fields, women immigrants from India seek and prefer workplaces that are diverse. In contrast to earlier findings regarding co-ethnic bonding among, for example, Indian taxi drivers in New York, we find that professional women are not necessarily interested in workplaces with many Indians.[12] Our respondents tended to believe that organizations with an international workforce would be more equipped to recognize cultural differences and the specific skills that they brought to the table. This finding begs the question as to why certain groups of immigrants – for example, taxi drivers from Punjab – prefer to work with co-ethnics while others, such as women in STEM or women academics, do not. In part, this is linked to a sense that Indian men dominate the professional immigrant Indian landscape. As Ragini, Kavita and Shobha recounted, there are considerable tensions and disconnects between Indian men and women in the US. Additionally, such variations in the preferences and priorities within a given immigrant group could be a fruitful area for future research.

Leaning in and reaching out

Padmasree Warrior has noted that, when she first started working, she felt daunted by the fact that she had very few female colleagues. Our respondents expressed similar concerns about building social capital in unfamiliar work environments. Padma came to the United States with significant work experience. She went on to acquire a graduate degree from a prestigious institution in the United States. Nonetheless, she feels that her company, while diverse, has a "boys club," a "buddy buddy thing" that has "not impacted my work [till now], but might impact my growth." The barriers encountered from being both relatively new to the United States and from being a woman result in some challenging intersections.

In an interview to an Indian newspaper in 2007, Nooyi recollected that, early in her career, she realized that business conversations in the US often involved references to sporting events and the use of sports metaphors. She, therefore, decided to build her understanding of baseball, which is similar in its "bat and ball" format to the Indian favorite, cricket.[13] The question of sports banter came up frequently in our interviews. Some women mentioned that they skim sports magazines so that they can participate, if only superficially, in office conversations. Others, such as Mahi and Vani, felt that they could not fake an interest in sports at their age.[14] Mahi believes that those who can relate to baseball, basketball or American football have a distinct advantage in networking. Bidisha recalls being flummoxed by the frequent usage of the term "inside baseball" by her colleagues. It took her a few weeks to understand that the term referred to office politics.

Of course, the very presence of a diverse workforce can, over time, serve to alter workplace protocols, norms and environment. In Shobha's story, we see the importance of proactive organizational support. She mentioned,

> I had realized, during my layoff, that networks are the most important thing. These networks were very important . . . [joining associations that work with women and with professionals from the Asia-Pacific region] made me self-aware. For example, [we] talked about how Asians smile and lot and don't say no easily. We talked about how both these mannerisms, which are cultural, can be interpreted wrongly. Once you are aware, you can neutralize [the miscommunication].

Deborah also noted that active networking, facilitated by her organization, was key to professional growth. On the other hand, Shobha and Kavita both observed that Indians are more individualistic in building their career; they tend not to seek out the support of networks. Vani says that she was unable to find any associations that helped women like her, who were older, experienced professionals at the time of their arrival in the US. Overall, those who came to the United States as students found it easier to build social networks that then translated to professional contacts, as compared to women, like Vani and Mahi, who came to the country as older professionals.

Family life

Most, but not all, of the women we interviewed married someone of their choice rather than someone that their family chose. Most of the respondents made the decision to marry after having immigrated to the US. Sonali, Asha and Puja were notable exceptions to this. They came to the US after having been married and having had children.[15] Almost all of the women we interviewed noted that they chose the time of their marriage, usually after having established themselves in their career. Our respondents were keenly aware of the pressures that women in India face to get married young and made the conscious decision to resist that pressure. Ragini, for example, remembers that her family in India would often raise the issue of marriage with her. "By then, I had become emancipated. I held the cards in *my* [emphasis added] hand, since I was a half-world away." The views of our respondents about choosing their partners were articulated most explicitly by Anita. She was emphatic in asserting that a woman who is able to choose her life partner should consciously find someone who is supportive of her professional aspirations and ambitions. Uma, Reena, Mira and others mentioned that they had seen their relatives and friends get married at a young age and made the conscious decision to make a different choice. An early marriage, in their view, would restrict their professional and personal mobility. When they did get married, our respondents worked hard to ensure equality of work responsibilities with their spouses.

Radhika, for example, married a man who was introduced to her through family and who belongs to the same community as she does. She says that her husband has always been supportive of her career. She asserts, with palpable pride, that " I have not made any compromises on my career, except my own decision to cut back on my work hours after having children." Shobha had an arranged marriage after she had been working for a few years in the US. She and her husband decided to both pursue full-time jobs and MBAs while raising a young child. She recalls,

> I would go to classes [at graduate school] some days a week, and my husband would go other days. . . . We worked around [our daughter's] daycare schedule. We would take turns with her . . . she is used to being raised by one parent at a time.

Shobha and her spouse eventually decided to relocate to another city after completing their MBA programs. Shobha found a job first. After their relocation, her husband was the primary caregiver for their child, till he, too, found full-time employment. Now, they share childcare responsibilities based on their work schedules. In the affirmative story that Shobha recounts, and in the more contentious stories of some of our other respondents, we encounter the micropolitics of challenging conventional norms about family life.

We should remember, of course, that these micropolitics lead to considerable contention as well. As we noted earlier in the book, Ragini encountered societal skepticism about her career priorities after she got married. In an earlier chapter, we had discussed Mahi, who had migrated to the US in her thirties. She has found it difficult to relate to Indian men. "I stay away from Indian men," she said, due to what she perceives are their problematic assumptions about her. Asha and Sonali both had considerable conflicts in their marriages, in part due to their professional choices. Many of our contacts reflected on the reluctance of Indian men to help out with childcare and household work.

Twice blessed

Vijay Prashad had famously said that professional Indian Americans are "twice blessed."[16] The first blessing was to have been born in post-independence India. The second was to have been born during or after the civil rights movement in the United States, which enabled the enactment of the 1965 Hart-Cellar Act. This act made it possible for Indians to work and live in the US, something that was unlikely in the pre-1965 decades, given the discriminatory nature of US policy towards immigrants from Asia. Both these blessings came with multiple and complex layers. In India, state policy consciously made education available to Indians, regardless of class, gender, caste, or linguistic barriers. The availability of education is not, however, the same as accessibility of education. Persistent socio-economic inequalities have made education in English and higher education – both important determinants of professional success in India – the domain of a minority of India's overall population. While the education system in post-independence India has never discriminated on the basis of gender, women still face considerable barriers to availing of educational facilities. It is not surprising, therefore, that most of our respondents do not perceive or seek common ground with Indian immigrant men. They believe that men, due to a variety of societal factors in both countries, have an advantage in charting their professional journeys.

Looking beyond the independent visa category

Our study would be remiss if we were to not recognize that many women come to the US from India on dependent (usually spousal) visas and then go on to build careers of their own. One of our respondents noted that her sisters had come to the country with their husbands and had gone on to build successful careers. In a number of discussions that we had with both men and women about our research, we were reminded that not everyone's immigrant professional pathway begins with an independent visa. It should also be noted that, till mid-2015, those who arrived on a dependent visa faced strong restrictions to working in the United States. As a part of President's Obama 2015 Executive Order on immigration, the Department of Homeland Security began to allow certain dependent spouses of H-1B visa holders who are seeking employment-based lawful permanent resident status to seek and accept employment.[17] Interestingly, in some immigrant circles, the H-4 visas, which are provided to dependent spouses and children, are called "depression visas" or a "golden cage" because holders had not been permitted to work outside the home.[18]

In the course of our research, we interviewed five women who arrived in the US on dependent visa categories. While they are not part of our main sample base, the professional journeys of these women provide some fascinating insights, which we recount here. Naina is a tenured professor at a large state university. After having an arranged marriage at a young age, she arrived in the US on a H-4 spousal visa. Faced with visa-related barriers to finding employment, she decided to apply to doctoral programs in the US. Naina eventually completed her PhD from a prestigious university and achieved significant professional success at one of the top-ranked universities in her discipline. Reflecting on her initially journey to the US, she said, "I was not big on coming to the US, but I knew I wanted to study more and I knew I could not work and study in India while being married to a man from my community there." Like Uma, Naina came from a socially conservative business family where there was little emphasis on education in general and education for girls in particular. Unlike the majority of the women whom we interviewed, including Uma, she faced strong family opposition to her decision to pursue higher studies and employment. Reflecting on her professional achievements, Naina says that "When I started working . . . I saw that, for the first time, I was in a meritocracy. In my upbringing, girls were just put in a corner. But, now, I was being recognized for my work." Notwithstanding her successes in the workplace, she feels a sense of alienation from other Indian professional women. Naina believes that her identity as a woman who comes from a socially conservative family has excluded her from groups that, in her opinion, represent the interests of "elite, educated Indian women." She said,

> I think Indian women who come from educated families, where, unlike me, they were encouraged to study . . . judge me . . . The sophisticated women, they demote me for my family background, my clothes,

my desire to speak in Hindi. . . . They don't want to give me a seat at their table.

Naina's experiences speak to some interesting and understudied dimensions and nuances of women's education and professional advancement in India. She comes from a wealthy but very conservative family where gender roles have remained firmly bounded. In contrast to most of our subjects, her professional aspirations were not supported by older women in her family. Perhaps because of these differences, she feels that she has not been able to find a cohort of Indian professional woman with whom she can talk about "how to manage personal identities and work."

Kajal, who arrive in the US on a J-2 dependent visa, had a different experience. While she also came from a socially conservative business family in India, her parents did not oppose her interest in acquiring academic credentials in the sciences. She married a man whom she met while pursuing her undergraduate degree in India. It was his decision and motivation to move to the US. Unlike our independent migrants, Kajal was not particularly motivated to leave India and move overseas. At the same time, she notes that "I always knew I was going to study and work in the US. I took my GRE, TOEFL, and Subject GRE before coming to the US." Her professional choices were supported by her then fiancé and now husband. She recalled,

> My husband was very supportive. He was in the US before me, and he brought back the Subject GRE books. In those days, those books were hard to find in India, so it was very helpful for me. I also shared those books with some of my friends in India, who were also doing their subject GRE.

Now working at a start-up, Kajal is strongly motivated to work with Indian women in helping them pursue fulfilling careers. She has pursued this through active involvement in organizations promoting the presence and success of Indian women in business and the sciences.

> I think there is a lack of awareness among Indian women and what they can do and what others have done. It's really inspiring to listen to women entrepreneurs, the risk they have taken. As an immigrant, you hesitate to take risks because half your time goes waiting for your green card and then maybe you forget what you wanted to do after you got that card. . . . So, I want to [contribute to efforts that] inspire and motivate. I want women to find the mentors they need to strike out on their own.

Unlike Naina and Kajal, Sapna, who arrived in the US on a dependent family visa in 1973, had no professional aspirations at all. Yet today she has a demanding career as a full-time employee of a large multinational company. How did Sapna make this journey? When she arrived in the US, Sapna was a young widow. "I was so young and unexposed," she recollects.

I had no expectations of the US. . . . [My family was paying] for me to go to school, but I wasn't taking it very seriously. One day, my brother in law said he didn't want to keep wasting money on my studies if I wasn't interested. . . . if I wanted to do more, then I had to study. That sunk in like a rock.

Here, as with many of our respondents, the encouragement of family proved to be very important for Sapna. As she progressed in her career, Sapna encountered many of the challenges that our independent women immigrants witnessed. She said,

Overall, I think I could have done better. If I was two sizes lighter, I could have gone further. I think outward appearance is very important here. How you groom, dress. You have to dress and behave like a professional and white woman. . . . [Nowadays] companies like mine [discuss] diversity and inclusion. Then, you have to be different enough to qualify but not too different. If I showed up with a bindi on my head, that would be too different. . . . Basically, you need to be thin, groomed, walk the walk and talk the talk. That's corporate America.

It is notable that Sapna arrived with significant family support in the US and with no career interests. Yet her journey reflects, in some significant ways, those of our primary cohort.

The struggles of Naina, Kajal and Sapna also illustrate a different set of micropolitics – of arriving here with a dependent identity yet forging a distinct professional space for themselves. While a further exploration of these issues is beyond the scope of our study, we hope that our findings encourage further research on the varied journeys that immigrant women have undertaken to build up their careers in the US.

The path ahead

In the preceding pages and chapters, we have chronicled a number of stories of women who have embarked on challenging and rewarding journeys to the US in pursuit of productive professional and personal lives. Embedded in these narratives is also the larger story of two countries, the US and India, and their evolving engagement with issues of gender equality. Viewed through the lens of the independent immigrant women's experiences, we are able to see the links between the everyday lived experiences of boundary-pushing decisions and the larger systemic and organized changes in the gender landscape in both countries. At the same time, we have also shown that the individual determination of women immigrants from India has been supported by societal changes to create remarkable stories of resilience and spirit that in turn carries forward the processes of change.

Uma reflected on how unusual it was for a woman of her generation and circumstances to travel alone to the US to pursue graduate studies and build an impressive career as a scientist: "Only later was I able to appreciate my luck in that I was able to slip through the crack." She is also acutely aware that luck and individual grit were not the only aids to her journey. Remembering the many who supported and enabled her, she emphasizes that it was more than just luck that helped her journey. "I stand on the shoulders of the women who came before me," she said, "and my shoulders are ready to hold [others] up." In different ways, each of the women we have chronicled has reached higher, so as to enable themselves, and those who come after, to forge a stronger, firmer path forward.

Notes

1 National Aeronautics and Space Administration. "Biographical Data." http://www.jsc.nasa.gov/Bios/htmlbios/chawla.html (accessed April 15, 2015).
2 Waldman, Amy. 2003. "For Resolute Girl, the Traditions of India Imposed No Limits." *New York Times*, February 3: A1.
3 The Indian government has also recognized Chawla's contributions as a space researcher of Indian origin. The reputed Indian Institute of Technology at Kharagpur, for example, has a Kalpana Chawla Space Technology Cell.
4 Warrior stepped down from her role as CTO at Cisco in 2015. In December 2015, she assumed the role of US CEO of NextEV, a Chinese electric car company.
5 Waldman 2003.
6 See, for example, Cheng, Roger. 2015. "Women in Tech: The Numbers Don't Add Up." *CNET*, May 6. http://www.cnet.com/news/women-in-tech-the-numbers-dont-add-up/ (accessed May 2, 2015); Khanna, Derek. 2013. "We Need More Women in Tech: The Data Prove It." *The Atlantic*, October 29. http://www.theatlantic.com/technology/archive/2013/10/we-need-more-women-in-tech-the-data-prove-it/280964/ (accessed May 4, 2015); and Gellman, Lindsay and Georgia Wells. 2016. "What's Holding Back Women in Tech." *The Wall Street Journal*, March 22. http://www.wsj.com/articles/whats-holding-back-women-in-tech-1458639004 (accessed May 4, 2015).
7 Gilpin, Lyndsey. 2014. "Cisco CTO Padmasree Warrior: Engineer, Artist, Business Leader, Sage." http://www.techrepublic.com/article/cisco-cto-padmasree-warrior-engineer-artist-business-leader-sage/; http://www.techrepublic.com/article/cisco-

cto-padmasree-warrior-engineer-artist-business-leader-sage/ (accessed May 10, 2015).

8 http://girlsinict.org/profiles-of-women-in-ICT/padmasree-warrior (accessed May 10, 2015).

9 Email correspondence with authors, March 20, 2015.

10 As author Aatish Taseer reminds us, in India, access to English remains restricted to a privileged minority: "[English] . . . has created a linguistic line as unbreachable as the color line once was in the United States." http://www.nytimes.com/2015/03/22/opinion/sunday/how-english-ruined-indian-literature.html (accessed May 15, 2015).

11 Nilekani, Nandan. 2007. "Personal Side of Indra Nooyi." *The Economic Times*. http://articles.economictimes.indiatimes.com/2007–02–07/news/28471801_1_indra-nooyi-nandan-nilekani-personal-side/2 (accessed May 20, 2015).

12 Mitra 2012.

13 Nandan 2007.

14 It should be noted that Indian men also encounter difficulties in understanding the particulars of American sports. Most of the women we encountered felt, however, that men have an easier time absorbing the jargon of sports.

15 Interestingly, both women say that the Indian student networks in their respective universities were very supportive. "I was older," recalled Sonali, "and I had a son. But they looked up to me, and they took care of me when I needed it."

16 Prashad, Vijay. 2001. *The Karma of Brown Folk*. Minneapolis, MN: University of Minnesota Press.

17 http://www.uscis.gov/news/dhs-extends-eligibility-employment-authorization-certain-h-4-dependent-spouses-h-1b-nonimmigrants-seeking-employment-based-lawful-permanent-residence (accessed May 25, 2015).

18 An Indian H-4 visa holder started a Facebook page called, "H4 Visas, A Curse" to build support for a change to the legal framework. A 2013 article in the widely read popular magazine *Marie Claire* also discussed this issue. http://www.marieclaire.com/politics/news/a8218/h4-visa-debate-beyond-borders (accessed May 27, 2015).

Appendix

Table A.1 Respondents*

Person	India				US		
	Age left India	Year of departure	Place of origin in India	Level of education at time of departure	Current level of education in US	Profession in the US	Place of residence in the US
Anita	25	2005	Delhi	Master's	Master's	Management consultant	West Coast
Asha	27	1990	Delhi	PhD	PhD	Academic	West Coast
Ayesha	26	2009	Bangalore	Bachelor's	Master's	Management consultant	Midwest
Deborah	21	1997	Chennai	Bachelor's	Master's	Corporate	Midwest
Jaya	22	1973	Mumbai	Bachelor's	Second bachelor's degree equivalent	Medical technology professional (retired)	West Coast
Kavita	26	2001	Mumbai	Master's	Master's	HR professional	West Coast
Mahi	31	2008	Kolkata	MBA	No additional degrees in the US	Banking	East Coast
Maryam	20	1970	Kerala	Nursing degree	Nursing certification	Nurse (retired)	East Coast
Mira	20	1985	Delhi	Master's	PhD	Academic	West Coast
Nilima	23	1984	Mumbai	MBBS	MS	Management consultant	Midwest
Puja	36	2006	Bangalore	BE	MBA	Management consultant	South
Padma	23	1980	Hyderabad	MBA	PhD	Academic	East Coast
Radhika	22	1993	Mumbai	Master's	Master's	Health care	Midwest
Ragini	25	1998	Bangalore	BSc, math and CS	MBA	Entrepreneur	Midwest
Ratna	24	1994	Pune	Bachelor's	PhD	Technology	West Coast
Reena	26	1995	Delhi	Bachelor's	Bachelor's	Media	West Coast

Name	Age	Year	City	Education	Degree	Profession	Region
Rekha	21	1975	Mumbai	Master's	PhD	Academic	East Coast
Shanta	18	1982	Bangalore	High school	MBA	Marketing	East Coast
Shobha	24	1998	Pune	Master's	MBA	Health care Technology	West Coast
Sonali	32	2000	Mumbai	Master's	PhD	Academic	West Coast
Sujatha	25	2001	Hyderabad	BE	BE	Filmmaker	West Coast
Uma	20	1961	Mumbai	Bachelor's	PhD	Scientist (retired)	West Coast
Vani	38	1998	Pune	BE	MBA	Management consultant/IT consultant	Midwest

* All names have been changed to maintain the confidentiality of the responses. Ages are approximate.

Table A.2 The ancillary sample: respondents who arrived on dependent visas

Person	India				US		
	Age left India	Year of departure	Place of origin in India	Level of education at time of departure	Current level of education in US	Profession in the US	Place of residence in the US
Kajal	23	1995	Delhi	PhD	Master's	Scientist	West Coast
Kanya	21	1997	Chennai	Bachelor's	Master's	Corporate	Midwest
Naina	23	1999	Ahmedabad	Bachelor's	PhD	Academic	West Coast
Sapna	22	1973	Mumbai	Bachelor's	Bachelor's degree	Corporate	Southwest
Vinita	26	2001	Mumbai	Master's	Master's	HR professional	West Coast

Women immigrants from India: questionnaire

A. General biographical information

1) Age: Current and at migration.
2) Education: Education completed in India and the US.
3) Current occupation (prompt, if currently unemployed, if they have actively sought work in the past one month).
4) Marital status: Current and at the time of migration.
5) Place of residence in India, prior to migration.
6) Number of children, if any.
7) Immediate family (siblings, parents, children, other dependents) in India.
8) Nature of residence prior to migration: Family home, own place.
   a Did you live independently prior to coming to US? If so, under what conditions?
   b If you worked in India prior to arrival in the US, did you provide financial assistance at that time to your parents or other family members?
9) Years since migration to the US.

B. Questions related to the decision to migrate

1) For what purpose did you originally come to the US? What visa category did you come under?
2) Did you receive encouragement to consider migration from anyone – parents, other family, friends, teachers/mentors (in what way)?
3) If you came to the US to study, did you think academic opportunities were missing in India (for women)?
4) If you came to the US to work, did you think work opportunities in India were limiting (for women)?
5) Did financial reasons pay a part in your motivation? If so, were you seeking financial independence for yourself and/or financial security for your family in India?
6) In what ways, if at all, did you think your life would be better with migration?
7) Did you consider yourself or your decision feminist in anyway? Were you aware of a feminist movement in India?

C. Educational and occupation experience in the US

1) If you came to the US to study, how did you finance your studies?
2) If you came to the US to work, did you ever go back to school to study? How did you finance your study?

3) What motivated you to choose your field of study/work (if coming directly for employment)?

4) What was your experience like in the university? In what ways do you think your educational experience might have been different if you had continued in India?

5) How long did it take you to complete your education in the US?

6) If you made the transition from university to a job, can you briefly describe that choice and the transition experience?

7) Have you continued in the same field of work/education or have you made a transition(s) since coming to the US (explain)?

8) What barriers do you/did you encounter in maintaining your career in the US? Do you think these are different from the barriers you might have encountered in India?

9) Are you aware of the glass ceiling and the gender wage gap in the US economy? Do you feel you might have encountered a glass ceiling in the US?

10) In general what do you think are the challenges of working life for women in the US? Do you think there are challenges that are faced specifically by women immigrants? What about challenges faced specifically by women from India?

   a   Prompt on perceived status of Hispanic women, black women, East Asian women, South Asian women in comparison.

11) Do you feel financially more secure by being in the US?

12) Do you send money to your family in India or help them financially in anyway?

13) Do you feel your being in the US benefits/has benefitted your family in India? If so, in what way?

D. Social networks and race and gender

1) In your time as a student in the US (if applicable) did you join any social groups or associations? Can you tell us more about these associations and your experiences with them?

2) In your time as a working professional, have you joined any associations? Can you tell us about these associations and how, if at all, they have benefited your career progression?

3) Have you joined any associations or organizations outside of your student/professional interests? [Prompt here on South Asian groups, women's groups, other groups.] What were your experiences like with regard to these groups?

4) Are you aware of a feminist movement in the US? If so, explain. In what ways, if any, do you identify with this movement?

5) Have you heard of the term "women of color"? Whom might it refer to? Do you have any thoughts on the position of women of color in your industry/profession?

6) If you were married at the time of your entry into the US, can you explain how your professional and social interests were impacted by your spouse?

7) If you were single at the time of your entry into the US, did you have any experiences as a single woman that impacted your professional development? For example, did you seek out associations or organizations that addresses the professional the needs of single women or women in general (as opposed to co-educational organizations)?

    a   Did you face any pressure from your social community or family in India or the United States about your marital status? Did this impact your choices in terms of location in the US? Did it impact your professional choices in any other way?

8) If you are currently single, what impact do you think this has on your professional life here in the US?

E. Questions related to class in India

1) What income category does your family belong to in India (middle class, upper middle class, wealthy, lower middle class, lower income)? Can you explain why?

2) Mother's education?

3) Father's education?

4) Mother's occupation?

5) Father's occupation?

6) In India, what kinds of consumer durables did your family own at the time of your migration (e.g. fridge, TV, car)? Has that changed since you migrated? Have you helped family members, financially, since you migrated?

7) At the time of migration, did your family own or rent their home? Where was the home located?

8) Is there a caste that your family identifies with? Probe if the caste falls into any of the following reserved categories: SC/ST/OBC or if it is OC or privileged caste status. Did your caste or religious affiliation influence your decision to migrate? If so, why?

References

Adichie, Chimamanda Ngozi Adichie. 2010. *That Thing Around Your Neck*. New York: Anchor.

Adichie, Chimamanda Ngozi Adichie. 2014. *Americanah*. New York: Anchor.

Aguirre, DeAnne and Karim Sabbagh. 2010. "The Third Billion." *Strategy+Business*. http://www.strategy-business.com/article/10211?gko=98895 (accessed May 14, 2016).

American Community Survey. 2012. Available through the United States Census Bureau, www.census.gov.

An Act to Establish an Uniform Rule of Naturalization. 1790. 1st Cong., 2d Sess., Chap. 3.

Anandibai Joshi to Alfred Jones. 1883, June 28. *Materials Related to Rachel Bodley 1868–1991*. Drexel University College of Medicine, The Legacy Center Archives and Special Collections (a291_006).

Artsalt.com. 2014. "Q&A: Chimamanda Ngozi Adiche Tackles Race from African Perspective in 'Americanah'." March 4. http://www.artsatl.com/2014/03/qa-chimamanda-ngozi-adichie-americanah/ (accessed December 10, 2014).

Banerjee, Payal. 2006. "Indian Information Technology Workers in the United States: The H-1B Visa, Flexible Production, and the Racialization of Labor." *Critical Sociology* 32 (2–3): 425–445.

Bennett, Marion T. 1966. "The Immigration and Nationality (McCarran-Walter) Act of 1952, as Amended to 1965." *Annals of the American Academy of Political and Social Science* 367 (September): 127–136.

Bhatia, Sunil. 2007. *American Karma: Race, Politics, and Identity in the Indian Diaspora*. New York: New York University Press.

Caltech Archives. 2013. "Facts About Caltech History." http://archives.caltech.edu/about/fastfacts.html (accessed December 5, 2014).

Carr, David. 2005. "Will the Simpsons' Ever Age." *New York Times*. http://www.nytimes.com/2005/04/24/arts/television/24carr.html?pagewanted=1 (accessed June 2, 2014).

Celarent, Barbara. 2011. "The High Caste Hindu Woman. Rev. of *Pandita Ramabai's America: Conditions of Life in the United States (United Stateschi Lokasthiti ani Pravasvritta)*." *American Journal of Sociology* 117 (1): 353–360.

Census of India. 2011. "Provisional Population Totals: India: Census 2011." http:// censusindia.gov.in/2011-prov-results/indiaatglance.html (accessed June 2, 2014).

Chakravarti, Uma. 1998. *Rewriting History: The Life and Times of Pandita Ramabai.* New Delhi: Kali for Women.

Chakravarty, Paula. 2006. "Symbolic Analysts or Indentured Servants? Indian High-Tech Migrants in America's Information Economy." *Knowledge, Technology & Policy* 19 (3): 27–43.

Chakravarty, Anuradha. 2013. "Political Science and the 'Micro-Politics' Research Agenda." *Journal of Political Sciences and Public Affairs* 1 (1): e103.

Cheng, Roger. 2015. "Women in Tech: The Numbers Don't Add Up." *CNET*, May 6. http://www.cnet.com/news/women-in-tech-the-numbers-dont-add-up/ (accessed May 2, 2014).

Chitnis, Suma. 2004. "Feminism: Indian Ethos and Indian Convictions." In *Feminism in India*, ed. Maitrayee Chaudhuri. New Delhi: Kali for Women, 8–25.

Congregational Library. "Dr. Gurubai Karmarkar, M.D." *Congregational Library Exhibits.* http://exhibits.congregationallibrary.org/items/show/105 (accessed May 31, 2014).

Cotter, David A., Joan M. Hermsen, Seth Ovadia, and Reeve Vanneman. 2001. "The Glass Ceiling Effect." *Social Forces* 80 (2): 655–681.

Dasgupta, Shamita Das. 1998. *A Patchwork Shawl: Chronicles of South Asian Women in America.* New Brunswick: Rutgers University Press.

Department of Commerce. 2011. "Women in STEM: A Gender Gap to Innovation." http://www.esa.doc.gov/sites/default/files/womeninstemagaptoinnovation8311. pdf (accessed December 15, 2014).

Department of Homeland Security. 2013. "Characteristics of H1-B Specialty Occupation Workers, Fiscal Year 2012 Annual Report to Congress." http://www.uscis. gov/sites/default/files/USCIS/Resources/Reports%20and%20Studies/H-1B/h1b-fy-12-characteristics.pdf (accessed December 20, 2014).

Dhingra, Pawan. 2007. *Managing Multicultural Lives: Asian American Professionals and the Challenges of Multiple Identities.* Palo Alto, CA: Stanford University Press.

Ehrenreich, Barbara, and Arlie Russel Hochschild. 2002. *Global Woman: Nannies, Maids and Sex Workers in the New Economy.* New York: Henry Holt.

Eileen, Pollack. 2013. "Why Are There Still So Few Women in Science?" *New York Times*, October 3. http://www.nytimes.com/2013/10/06/magazine/why-are-there-still-so-few-women-in-science.html?pagewanted=all&_r=0 (accessed December 21, 2014).

Faludi, Susan. 1991. *Backlash: The Undeclared War Against American Women.* New York: Crown.

Faludi, Susan. 2013. "Facebook Feminism, Like It or Not." *The Baffler 23.* http:// www.thebaffler.com/salvos/facebook-feminism-like-it-or-not (accessed January 18, 2015).

Federal Glass Ceiling Commission. 1995. "A Solid Investment: Making Full Use of the Nation's Human Capital." http://www.dol.gov/dol/aboutdol/history/reich/ reports/ceiling2.pdf (accessed December 1, 2014).

Ferber, Marianne A. and Julie A. Nelson. 1993. *Beyond Economic Man: Feminist Theory and Economics*. Chicago: University of Chicago Press.

Forbes, Geraldine. 1994. "Medical Careers and Health Care for Indian Women: Patterns of Control." *Women's History Review* 3 (4): 515–530.

Friedan, Betty. 1963. *The Feminine Mystique*. New York: W.W. Norton.

Fruzetti, Lina M. 1993. *The Gift of a Virgin: Women, Marriage, and Ritual in a Bengali Society*. New Delhi: Oxford University Press.

GeekWire. 2014. "Internal Memo: Microsoft CEO Satya Nadella Sets New Diversity Plan After 'Humbling' Experience." October 15. http://www.geekwire.com/2014/internal-memo-microsoft-ceo-sets-new-diversity-plan-humbling-experience/ (accessed December 27, 2014).

Gellman, Lindsay and Georgia Wells. 2016. "What's Holding Back Women in Tech." *The Wall Street Journal*, March 22. http://www.wsj.com/articles/whats-holding-back-women-in-tech-1458639004 (accessed May 4, 2014).

George, Sheba. 2005. *When Women Come First: Gender and Class in Transnational Migration*. Berkeley: University of California Press.

Gilpin, Lyndsey. 2014. "Cisco CTO Padmasree Warrior: Engineer, Artist, Business Leader, Sage." http://www.techrepublic.com/article/cisco-cto-padmasree-warrior-engineer-artist-business-leader-sage/; http://www.techrepublic.com/article/cisco-cto-padmasree-warrior-engineer-artist-business-leader-sage/ (accessed May 10, 2014).

Godbole, Rohini. 2008. "It's Been an Interesting Journey." In *Lilavati's Daughters: The Women Scientists of India*, eds. Rohini Godbole and Ram Ramaswamy. Bangalore: Indian Academy of Sciences, 110–113.

Government of India. 1958. "Scientific Policy Resolution 1958." http://dst.gov.in/stsysindia/spr1958.htm (accessed December 30, 2015).

Guha Ghosal, Sarbani. 2005. "Major Trends of Feminism in India." *The Indian Journal of Political Science* LXVI (4): 793–812.

Gurjarpadhye, Prachi. 2014. "Through a Changing Feminist Lens Three Biographies of Anandibai Joshi." *Economic & Political Weekly* 49 (33): 37–40.

Halley, Jean, Amy Eshleman, and Ramya Mahadevan Vijaya. 2011. *Seeing White: An Introduction to White Privilege and Race*. Lanham, MD: Rowman & Littlefield.

Herzog, Hanna. 2009. "Choice as Everyday Politics: Female Palestinian Citizens of Israel in Mixed Cities." *International Journal of Politics, Culture, and Society* 22 (1): 5–21.

Hira, Ron. 2010. "The H-1B and L-1 Visa Programs Out of Control." *Economic Policy Institute Briefing Paper No. 280*.

Hondagneu-Sotelo, Pierrette. 2003. *Gender and U.S. Immigration: Contemporary Trends*. Berkeley: University of California Press.

Hondagneu-Sotelo, Pierrette. 2007. *Domestica: Immigrant Workers Cleaning and Caring in the Shadows of Affluence*. Berkeley: University of California Press.

hooks, bell. 2000. *Feminist Theory: From Margin to Center*. Boston: South End Press.

Hyun, Jane. 2005. *Breaking the Bamboo Ceiling*. New York: Harper Collins.

Indian National Science Academy. 2001. *Pursuit and Promotion of Science: The Indian Experience.* New Delhi: INSA.

International Labour Organization. 2013. *Global Employment Trends 2013.* Geneva: International Labour Organization.

International Labour Organization. 2013. "India: Why Is Women's Labour Force Participation Dropping?" *ILO Newsroom,* 13 February. http://www.ilo.org/global/about-the-ilo/newsroom/comment-analysis/WCMS_204762/lang – en/index.htm?utm_source=twitterfeed&utm_medium=twitter

Kabeer, Naila. 2001. *The Power to Choose: Bangladeshi Garment Workers in London and Dhaka.* London: Verso.

Kalita, Mitra. 2005. *Suburban Sahibs.* New Brunswick: Rutgers University Press.

Kennedy, Edward M. 1966. "The Immigration Act of 1965." *Annals of the American Academy of Political and Social Science* 367 (September): 137–149.

Khanna, Derek. 2013. "We Need More Women in Tech: The Data Prove It." *The Atlantic,* October 29. http://www.theatlantic.com/technology/archive/2013/10/we-need-more-women-in-tech-the-data-prove-it/280964/ (accessed May 5, 2014).

Kirkegaard, Jacob Funk. 2007. "The Accelerating Decline in America's High-Skilled Workforce: Implications for Immigration Policy." *Policy Analysis in International Economics, Institute for International Economics No. 84.*

Kosambi, Meera. 1996. "Anandibai Joshee: Retrieving a Fragmented Feminist Image." *Economic and Political Weekly* 31 (49): 3189–3197.

Kosambi, Meera. 2002. "Returning the American Gaze Pandita Ramabai's the Peoples of the United States, 1889." *Meridians* 2 (2): 188–212.

Koutin, Mawuva Remarque. 2015. "Why Are White People Expats While the Rest of Us Are Immigrants?" *The Guardian.* http://www.theguardian.com/global-development-professionals-network/2015/mar/13/white-people-expats-immigrants-migration (accessed December 30, 2015).

Krishna, Anirudh and Devendra Bajpai. 2015. "Layers in Globalising Society and the New Middle Class in India Trends, Distribution and Prospects." *Economic & Political Weekly* 50 (5): 69–77.

Lahiri, Jhumpa. 2003. *The Namesake.* New York: Houghton Mifflin.

Lahiri, Jhumpa. 2009. *Unaccustomed Earth.* New York: Vintage.

Lahiri, Jhumpa. 2013. *The Lowland.* New York: Knopf.

Liu, John, M. 1992. "The Contours of Asian Professional, Technical and Kindred Work Immigration, 1965–1988." *Sociological Perspectives* 35 (4): 673–704.

Marston, Ama. 2013. "Are Women in the West Being Left Behind on Leadership?" *The Guardian.* http://www.theguardian.com/women-in-leadership/2013/oct/23/women-in-west-left-behind-leadership (accessed May 5, 2014).

McGuire, Gail M. 2002. "Gender, Race, and the Shadow Structure: A Study of Informal Networks and Inequality in a Work Organization." *Gender and Society* 16 (3): 303–322.

Mitra, Diditi. 2012. "Social Capital Investment and Immigrant Economic Trajectories: A Case Study of Punjabi American Taxi Drivers in New York City." *International Migration* 50 (4): 67–84.

Mohanty, Chandra Talpade. 1984. "Under Western Eyes: Feminist Scholarship and Colonial Discourses." *Boundary 2* 12 (13): 333–358.

Mohanty, Chandra Talpade. 2003. "'Under Western Eyes' Revisited: Feminist Solidarity through Anticapitalist Struggle." *Signs* 28 (2): 499–535.

Mouw, Ted. 2003. "Social Capital and Finding a Job: Do Contacts Matter?" *American Sociological Review* 68 (6): 868–898.

National Aeronautics and Space Administration. "Biographical Data." http://www. jsc.nasa.gov/Bios/htmlbios/chawla.html (accessed April 15, 2015).

National Public Radio. 2014. "Does the 'Bamboo Ceiling' Shut Asian Americans Out of Top Jobs?" May 23. http://www.npr.org/2014/05/23/315129852/does-a-bamboo-ceiling-shut-asian-americans-out-of-top-jobs (accessed December 5, 2014).

New York Times. 1888. "The Pandita Speaking on Behalf of Her Sisters." February 17.

Nilekani, Nandan. 2007. "Personal Side of Indra Nooyi." *The Economic Times*. http://articles.economictimes.indiatimes.com/2007–02–07/news/28471801_1_indra-nooyi-nandan-nilekani-personal-side/2 (accessed May 20, 2015).

Passar, Patricia R. 2003. "Engendering Migration Studies: The Case of New Immigrants in the United States." In *Gender and U.S. Immigration: Contemporary Trends*, ed. Pierrette Hondagneu-Sotelo. Berkeley: University of California Press, 20–43.

Prashad, Vijay. 2001. *The Karma of Brown Folk.* Minneapolis, MN: University of Minnesota Press.

Putnam, Robert. 1994. *Making Democracy Work: Civic Traditions in Modern Italy.* Princeton, NJ: Princeton University Press.

Rosenzweig, Eric. 2010. "Finding Aid Rachel L. Bodley Papers." Philadelphia Area Consortium of Special Collections Library. 24 July. http://hdl.library.upenn. edu/1017/d/pacscl/DUCOM_WMSC420xml (accessed April 25, 2014).

Rufus, Carl W. 1942. "Twenty-Five Years of the Barbour Scholarships." *Michigan Alumnus Quarterly Review* 49 (11): 14–26.

Sandberg, Sheryl. 2013. *Lean in: Women, Work, and the Will to Lead.* New York: Knopf.

Sen, Samita. 2000. "Toward a Feminist Politics? The Indian Women's Movement in Historical Perspective." *The World Bank Policy Research Report on Gender and Development Working Paper Series No. 9.*

Shah, Sonia. 1998. "Three Hot Meals and a Full Day at Work." In *A Patch Work Shawl: Chronicles of South Asian Women in America*, ed. Shamita Das Gupta. New Brunswick: Rutgers University Press, 206–222.

Shukla, Rajesh. 2010. *How India Earns, Spends and Saves – Unmasking the Real India.* SAGE and New Delhi: NCAER.

Slaughter, Anne-Marie. 2012. "Why Women Can't Have It All." *The Atlantic*, July/ August.

Slaughter, Anne-Marie. 2015. *Unfinished Business: Women, Work, Family.* New York: Random House.

Subramanian, C.V. 2008. "Edavaleth Kakkat Janaki Ammal." In *Lilavati's Daughters: The Women Scientists of India*, eds. Rohini Godbole and Ram Ramaswamy. Bangalore: Indian Academy of Sciences, 1–4.

Taseer, Aatish. 2015. "How English Ruined Indian Literature." *The New York Times*, March 19. http://www.nytimes.com/2015/03/22/opinion/sunday/how-english-ruined-indian-literature.html (accessed May 15, 2015).

United Nations Development Programme. 2013. *Human Development Report 2013*. New York: United Nations Development Programme.

United States Census Bureau. 2012. "2012 American Community Survey 1-Year Estimates, Table B05006." http://factfinder2.census.gov (accessed June 8, 2014).

United States Census Bureau. 2013. "2013 American Community Survey 1-Year Estimates, Table B05006." http://factfinder2.census.gov (accessed June 8, 2014).

Urry, Meg. 2005. "Diminished by Discrimination We Scarcely See." *Washington Post*, February 6. http://www.washingtonpost.com/wp-dyn/articles/A360–2005Feb5.html (accessed December 22, 2014).

Vijaya, Ramya and Hema Swaminathan. 2015. "Engendering the Economic Measurement of Middle Class: Evidence from India." Presentation to the Eastern Economics Association Conference, February, New York.

Waldman, Amy. 2003. "For Resolute Girl, the Traditions of India Imposed No Limits." *New York Times*, February 3: A1.

Walker, Rebecca. 1992. "Becoming the Third Wave." *Ms.*

Washington Post. 2014. "Microsoft CEO's Remarks about Raises Shouldn't Just Be Unsettling to Women." October 10. http://www.washingtonpost.com/blogs/on-leadership/wp/2014/10/10/microsoft-ceos-remarks-about-raises-shouldnt-just-be-unsettling-to-women/ (accessed December 26, 2014).

Webley, Kayla. 2013. "Beyond Borders," *Marie Claire*. http://www.marieclaire.com/politics/news/a8218/h4-visa-debate-beyond-borders/

Woman's Board of Missions. 1911. *Life and Light for Woman*. Boston: Frank Wood.

World Economic Forum. 2013. *The Global Gender Gap Report 2013*. Geneva: World Economic Forum.

Yang, Wesley. 2011. "Paper Tigers: What Happens to All the Asian–American Overachievers When the Test-Taking Ends?" *New York Magazine*, May 3. http://nymag.com/news/features/asian-americans-2011–5/ (accessed December 7, 2014).

Zlotnik, Hania. 2003. "The Global Dimensions of Female Migration." *Migration Information Source*. Migration Policy Institute. http://www.migrationpolicy.org/article/global-dimensions-female-migration (accessed April 1, 2016).

Zong, Jie and Jeanne Batalova. 2015. "Indian Immigrants in the United States." *Migration Information Source*. Migration Policy Institute http://www.migrationpolicy.org/article/indian-immigrants-united-states (accessed August 19, 2015).

Index